MWEN KA ALÉ

— *The* —
FRENCH-LEXICON CREOLE *of* GRENADA:
HISTORY, LANGUAGE *and* CULTURE

MWEN KA ALÉ
The French-lexicon Creole of Grenada: History, Language and Culture
Marise La Grenade-Lashley

© 2016 by Marise La Grenade-Lashley
Cover Photo of Rodney Peters, Moyah, St. Andrew's, Grenada. © 2013
Marise La Grenade-Lashley
Photos © Marise La Grenade-Lashley and Nnamdi Hodge

Published by Aventine Press
55 East Emerson St.
Chula Vista CA 91911
www.aventinepress.com

ISBN: 978-1-59330-903-9

Printed in the United States of America

All rights reserved. No part of this book or website may be reproduced or transmitted in any form or by any means without permission, excepting brief quotes used in connection with a review.

MWEN KA ALÉ

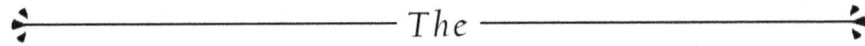

The FRENCH-LEXICON CREOLE *of* GRENADA:
HISTORY, LANGUAGE *and* CULTURE

MARISE LA GRENADE-LASHLEY

Contents

LIST OF ILLUSTRATIONS		vii
PREFACE		ix
ACKNOWLEDGEMENTS		xv
1.	GRENADA: GEOGRAPHY AND INDIGENOUS PEOPLE	1
	The Geography of Grenada	1
	Grenada's Indigenous People: The Kalinago	2
2.	COLONISATION, ENSLAVEMENT AND THE RISE AND FALL OF THE KÉYÒL LANGUAGE	11
	Kéyòl, Kwéyòl or Patois?	15
	The Origins of Grenada's Kéyòl	16
	The Rise and Fall of the Kéyòl Language in Grenada	21
	Factors behind the Decline of the Kéyòl Language in Grenada	26
	Geography	26
	Social Attitudes	27
	Education	30
	Religion and Colonial Rivalry	31
	Migration	36
	Grenada: A Hub of Activity	37
3.	MODERN-DAY KÉYÒL INFLUENCES IN GRENADA	39
	Grenadian English-lexicon Creole	39
	Storytelling and Folklore	42
	Proverbs and Idioms	43
	Folk Songs, Carnival and Calypso	47
	Religion and Spirituality	57
	Toponyms	58
	French-derived Toponyms in Grenada, Carriacou and Petite Martinique	58

4.	**LESSER ANTILLEAN FRENCH-LEXICON CREOLE: BASIC GRAMMAR**	**65**
	Historical Overview and Comparative Elements	65
	Pronunciation Guide: Vowels	68
	Oral Vowels	68
	Nasal Vowels	69
	Semi-vowels	69
	Pronunciation Guide: Consonants	69
	Personal Prounouns	71
	Subject Pronouns	71
	Object Pronouns	71
	The Possessive	72
	Articles	73
	Definite Article	73
	Indefinite Article	73
	Verb Tenses	74
	Present Tense	74
	Simple Past Tense	75
	Pluperfect Tense	75
	Imperfect Tense	76
	Immediate Future Tense	76
	Simple Future Tense	77
	Numbers	78
	Days of the Week	78
	Months of the Year	79
5.	**KÉYÒL RETENTIONS IN GRENADIAN ENGLISH-LEXICON CREOLE: GLOSSARY OF WORDS AND PHRASES**	**81**
	Notes on the Glossary	82
	Format of Glossary Entries	84
	Grenadian Kéyòl Glossary	86
6.	**REFERENCES**	**129**
7.	**FURTHER READING**	**133**

LIST OF ILLUSTRATIONS

1.1	The Leapers' Hill monument	7
1.2	The *roukou* plant (*Bixa orellana*)	9
2.1	Map of the parishes of Grenada	14
2.2	A *boli* (calabash) tree (*Crescentia cujete*)	19
3.1	A djab djab huddle on jouvé morning	51
3.2	A hooded vyéko dances to the stomping sound of his clogs	53
3.3	Signage for Duquesne Bay	60
3.4	Signage for the Perdmontemps Medical Station	62
5.1	The sugar cane plant (*Saccharum officinarum*)	86
5.2	A broom made from the bwa bouk tree	89
5.3	The bwa kano tree (*Cecropia schreberiana*)	91
5.4	The chado béni plant (*Eryngium foetidum*)	92
5.5	The dité péyi plant (*Capraria biflora*)	94
5.6	The flakoché fruit (*Flacourtia jangomas*)	97
5.7	The genn anba fèy plant (*Phyllanthus amarus*)	99
5.8	The kondisyon fruit (*Averrhoa bilimbi*)	106
5.9	Lambi (conch) shells	110
5.10	The latjé chat plant (*Acalypha hispida*)	111
5.11	The my hont plant (*Mimosa pudica*)	115
5.12	The piti bom plant (*Ocimum campechianum*)	117
5.13	The zèbapik plant (*Neurolaena lobata*)	125
5.14	The zèb zédri plant (*Bidens pilosa*)	127

PREFACE

The French-lexicon Creole title of this book, *Mwen Ka Alé*, translates as 'I am going'. This expression, which is used by Grenadian French-lexicon Creole lovers, serves as a poignant reminder that the French-lexicon Creole language is currently very much endangered in Grenada and will become extinct in the not-too-distant future. Losing a language is like losing one's cultural soul.

This book is intended to fill a void by documenting the history and evolution of Grenada's French-lexicon Creole language, the island's *lingua franca* for roughly 200 years, from the early 1700s to the early 1900s. It was only in the 1930s, roughly 85 years ago, that Grenada's French-lexicon Creole started to lose ground to English. Once the decline of this language had started, the process was remarkably swift. Currently, in 2016, the island's French-lexicon Creole speakers stand at a mere handful of elderly persons, a fact that added a sense of urgency to this project.

The terms 'Kéyòl' and Grenadian (or Grenada's) 'French-lexicon Creole' are used interchangeably in this book, with the term 'Kéyòl' being employed most of the time. The spelling 'Kéyòl' reflects the Grenadian pronunciation of the word 'Créole' using the Lesser Antillean French-lexicon Creole writing system adapted to Grenada. The decision to use the term 'Kéyòl' to refer to the language was not an easy or clear-cut one. Very few people, if any, in present-day Grenada would use the term 'Kéyòl' to refer to the island's French-lexicon Creole language. The term widely used and understood by Grenadians, particularly elderly Grenadians, remains 'Patois'. In fact, in the first draft of my book, I actually used the word 'Patois', despite being cognisant of its negative connotations. My reasoning at the time was that 'Patois' is the word still used by Grenadians, including Grenadian Kéyòl speakers, whose immeasurable contribution to Grenada's linguistic heritage is being honoured in this work, and that it would be somewhat artificial when writing a book about a language to refer to that language with a word other than that used by its speakers.

I also felt that, by writing 'Patois' with a capital <P>, I was granting it the same status as any other language. However, as the word 'patois' is of French origin, I decided to consult *Le Nouveau Petit Robert*, considered to be the most reliable modern French dictionary, for a detailed and thorough definition of this word. The one I found gave me pause. The extended definition of the word 'patois' is the following: *'Langue spéciale (considérée comme incorrecte ou incompréhensible)'* ['A particular way of speaking (considered incorrect or incomprehensible)'.] The word 'patois' originated in France and was first used to refer to rural varieties of French that differed from Standard French. As I thought about that definition in the Caribbean context, my thinking evolved, as it brought to mind the biased words once used by some to belittle or dismiss Creole languages in general, including French-lexicon Creole. I concluded that my use of the term 'Patois' in this book would serve to perpetuate or reinforce the myth of the innate inferiority of the language and, by extension, of its speakers, ultimately doing a disservice to the very language I was seeking to honour.

In the past, many Kéyòl speakers in Grenada were reluctant even to admit that they spoke the language because of negative societal attitudes to what was, in the minds of many, not even a language but instead simply corrupted French. Fortunately, attitudes are evolving in Grenada, and now that the language stands on the brink of extinction, there is a palpable sense of nostalgia among some in the elderly population when Kéyòl is discussed. The Lesser Antillean Anglophone islands of St. Lucia and Dominica, where this language is very much alive, deserve credit for helping shift attitudes towards their Kwéyòl[1] language by undertaking significant language development work. Indeed, the argument that Kéyòl is not a language is absurd: if people are able to use Kéyòl to communicate effectively day in and day out, it cannot be grammarless; there must be grammatical rules that govern its use and enable its speakers to understand each other, regardless of whether those rules have been codified or documented.

---

[1] The spelling used in St. Lucia and Dominica.

There are millions of French-lexicon Creole speakers worldwide, primarily in countries of the Americas and the Indian Ocean region. Haiti, a country with a population of 10 million, has the largest number of French-lexicon Creole (Kreyòl)[2] speakers. All Haitians speak French-lexicon Creole, with roughly 90 percent of the population being monolingual French-lexicon Creole speakers (only 10 percent of the population speaks French). When reviewing the history of French-lexicon Creole, a number of features emerge that are common to all its varieties: they developed over roughly the same period (1700 to 1800), they were largely developed by people of African ancestry and the majority of these peoples lived on islands.

Mention should also be made of the term 'pidgin', as French-lexicon Creole is sometimes incorrectly placed in this category. A pidgin arises when two linguistically different communities are thrust together and must find a way to communicate. A pidgin is used as the language of communication between two groups, but is not the first language of either group. In the case of a number of Caribbean islands that were once French possessions or under heavy French influence, French-lexicon Creole was, over differing time periods, the first and only language of the African population.

Although Grenada's Kéyòl stands on the brink of extinction as a language of everyday communication, it will live on in the cultural sphere, where commendable efforts are being made to preserve it in song. Furthermore, Kéyòl has placed more of an imprint on the tongues of Grenadians than we realise. Language is dynamic and ever-evolving and, over the years, many of Grenada's Kéyòl words have blended into Grenadian English and Grenadian English-lexicon Creole, many of the island's Kéyòl proverbs have been translated directly into English-lexicon Creole, and a host of place names, as well as the names of flora and fauna that hark back to Grenada's French- and Kéyòl-speaking era, have been retained.

This research effort was a painstaking one owing to the dearth of available information on Grenada's Kéyòl. In 1771 and 1775, major fires swept through the then wooden administrative buildings in St.

---

[2] The spelling used in Haiti.

George's, destroying important documents. Hurricanes devastated the island in 1955 and 2004, destroying a significant portion of the island's historical records in the process. In addition, insufficient attention has been paid over the years to the preservation of the island's historical documents. Against this backdrop, the contribution made by Grenada's Kéyòl speakers to this research project on the island's linguistic history and culture is priceless.

It is my hope that this book will generate interest, both in Grenada and beyond, in what will soon sadly become a lost language in Grenada, that it will inspire students to learn Kéyòl now that formal instruction is available in this language in neighbouring territories such as Trinidad & Tobago[3] and that it will encourage students to excel in the French language as they make the lexical connection between Kéyòl and French. It is also my fervent hope that by shedding light on Grenada's linguistic past, this book will give Grenadians a keener understanding of their history and heritage. For modern-day Grenadians, a people of predominantly African ancestry, Kéyòl is the first language spoken in Grenada by their ancestors. Few will deny that language is inextricably bound up with national identity. As one Kéyòl speaker movingly and forcefully told me during the course of my research, *'Patwa sé langay-nou'* ['Patois is our language'].

This book does not purport to be a linguistic study of Grenada's Kéyòl, nor does it examine what are considered to be the West African phonologies and grammatical structures that have influenced the language or form its substratum. A study of this nature would fall outside the author's scope of expertise. Instead, it examines the history of Grenada's Kéyòl and its lexical influence, which in this case is overwhelmingly exerted by the French language.

Mwen Ka Alé is a three-part book. The first part, broken down into three chapters, reviews the geography of Grenada and the immediate history of its native pre-colonial people, the Kalinago (Caribs), then goes on to trace the history and development of the Kéyòl language in Grenada, and lastly explores the reasons for its decline. A review is also offered of

---

[3] In Trinidad, as in Grenada, the term commonly used to refer to French-lexicon Creole is 'Patois'.

modern-day Kéyòl influences in Grenada as reflected in speech patterns, storytelling and folklore, proverbs and idioms, folk songs, carnival and calypso, and religion and spirituality.

The second part of this work, divided into two chapters, consists of an outline of the grammar of Lesser Antillean French-lexicon Creole adapted to Grenada, aimed at fostering a greater appreciation of this rich language, and an extensive glossary of Kéyòl word and phrase retentions in present-day Grenadian English-lexicon Creole, with their English equivalents and French etymology.

The third part is composed of audio-visual recordings made in 2013 and 2014 of Grenada's few remaining Kéyòl speakers. Readers can access these interviews through the *Mwen Ka Alé* video at mariselagrenadelashley.com. These interviews serve to illustrate and supplement some of the information provided in the book and, from the standpoint of Grenada's recorded history, are invaluable. It should be pointed out that, in the recorded conversations, the word 'Patois' was retained for ease of communication with its speakers, as it is the word to which they are accustomed.

ACKNOWLEDGEMENTS

It is with profound gratitude that I acknowledge the contribution made by the following Grenadian Kéyòl speakers, who generously and patiently shared their knowledge with me, answered my many questions and graciously agreed to be interviewed as part of this book project: Franklyn Bhola, Helen Charles, Edna Collins, Ana English, Myra Francis, Veronica 'Bedi' Jeremiah, Orleans John, Marcel Peters, Rodney Peters, Emmanuel Philip, Flodina Pierre (deceased) and Vernon Simon. Many of these Kéyòl speakers, who have the distinction of being the last remaining Kéyòl speakers on the island of Grenada, can be seen and heard in the *Mwen Ka Alé* video. Over time, these individuals have waged a quiet but determined struggle to preserve a dying language and, in so doing, have contributed immeasurably to the preservation of Grenada's culture.

I also owe a great debt of gratitude to Nnamdi Hodge, Merle Hodge, Merle Collins and the Society for Caribbean Linguistics. Without Nnamdi's help, this project may never have come to fruition. Nnamdi, a fluent French-lexicon Creole speaker who grew up in both Grenada and Trinidad & Tobago, provided assistance by selflessly taking time to interview and record the Kéyòl speakers featured on the *Mwen Ka Alé* video and to provide much of the technical expertise required to produce it. Merle Hodge, author of a number of critical works on Caribbean language, read the manuscript carefully and provided me with candid, incisive and wonderfully witty feedback. Merle Collins, a writer, friend and mentor, shared many useful insights with me and—no less important—both encouraged me to begin writing this book and prodded me to complete it. Members of the Executive Committee of the Society for Caribbean Linguistics provided valuable advice on the more technical aspects of the project.

MWEN KA ALÉ

Lastly, I wish to thank my relatives, particularly my nephew Allan La Grenade-Finch, who provided the technical assistance needed to create the video website (mariselagrenadelashley.com), as well as my sisters, husband and son, all of whom provided support in different but critical and loving ways.

1

GRENADA: GEOGRAPHY AND INDIGENOUS PEOPLE

The Geography of Grenada

The Caribbean Sea and its numerous islands collectively form what is known as the Caribbean. The tiny Caribbean island of Grenada, located in the south-eastern Caribbean Sea, is part of the archipelago of islands known as the Lesser Antilles. More specifically, Grenada is located north-west of the twin-island Republic of Trinidad & Tobago, north-east of Venezuela, and south-west of St. Vincent & the Grenadines. Grenada, a tri-island State, includes the much smaller islands of Carriacou and Petite Martinique. The combined land area of Grenada, Carriacou and Petite Martinique is roughly 133 square miles. Like most Caribbean islands, Grenada is an island of volcanic origin. The middle of the island is hilly and contains dense rainforest, while its jagged coastline harbours some of the world's finest beaches. The island's vegetation is lush and verdant owing to abundant rainfall. Its climate and fertile soil make it an ideal habitat for all manner of tropical plants, including a vast array of spices, the aroma of which wafts in the air in some parts of the island. Known as the 'Isle of Spice', Grenada is the world's second largest producer of nutmegs.

Grenada's picturesque capital, St. George's, is located in the south-western part of the island, in the parish bearing the same name. In the northern part of the island is the parish of St. Patrick, where Sauteurs, a town rich in history and symbolism, is located. The island has a total of six parishes.

Grenada's population currently stands at approximately 100,000. Its present-day inhabitants, a people of mainly African descent, were brought to the island's shores during the period of slavery, which spanned roughly 150 years, from the late 1600s to the early 1800s. Slavery was abolished in Grenada in 1834. Other ethnic groups in Grenada include persons of Kalinago (Carib), East Indian and European descent.

Although for linguistic purposes this study focuses on the period during which Africans were brought to Grenada's shores and on the development of the island's Kéyòl as a result of contact mainly between a number of West African languages and the language of European settlers, specifically the French, no study of Grenada's history, linguistic or otherwise, would be complete without an examination of the role and contributions of the island's indigenous people—the Kalinago—to Grenada as we know it today.

Grenada's Indigenous People: The Kalinago

Archaeological and linguistic data (Boomert 2003, 139-140) suggest that an ethnolinguistic group originally migrant from South America, speaking an Arawakan language, had been resident in the Lesser Antilles, including the island now known as Grenada, up to around 1400. The best reconstruction of this group's original name, 'Igneri' [Iñeri], is provided by Douglas Taylor (Taylor 1977, 14). In the decades after 1400, the 'Igneri' seem to have had contact with an incoming ethnolinguistic group speaking Kalina/Carib, also migrating from South America. The two communities merged, self-identifying as Kalinago. They spoke a language that, in structure and basic vocabulary, was largely the same as that of the preceding 'Igneri', but with an overlay of Kalina/Cariban vocabulary associated with the speech patterns of adult males (Boomert 2003, 146). It was this ethnic group that the Europeans encountered in the Lesser Antilles, which is when they gave them the name Caribs. Modern-day descendants of this population survive, minus their language, which died in the early twentieth century, in the Kalinago (Carib) communities and populations of St. Vincent and Dominica. In addition, there are the Garinagu people of Central America, with their Garifuna language intact, created by the British expulsion from St. Vincent to Central America in the late 1790s of a Kalinago community known as the 'Black Caribs' that resisted British occupation of St. Vincent. The indigenous people who once lived in Grenada, identified as Carib, are descendants of this broader Kalinago ethnolinguistic group that inhabited the Lesser Antilles at the end of the fifteenth century.

Petroglyphs produced hundreds of years ago by Grenada's indigenous people and located in the Duquesne Bay and Mt. Rich areas of the island serve as a modern-day reminder of the presence of these indigenous peoples in Grenada and their contributions to the island's culture.

Several failed attempts were made by Europeans in the early 1600s to settle in Grenada. In 1609, the British tried for the first time to establish a settlement in Grenada. A party of 200 arrived in three ships named Diana, Penelope and Endeavour. The Kalinago waged a relentless war on these settlers and ultimately forced them to abandon their efforts to settle there. In around 1638, a Frenchman named Philippe de Longvilliers de Poincy, twice appointed Governor of the French part of St. Kitts (St. Christopher) between 1639 and 1660, made plans to settle in Grenada. However, the island's distance from St. Kitts and the prospect of Kalinago resistance appear to have led him to rethink his plans.

The *Histoire Générale des Antilles Habitées par les François* [General History of the West Indies Inhabited by the French], written by Dominican missionary Jean-Baptiste du Tertre, states in reference to Grenada that:

> *Dèz[4] l'an 1638, M. de Poincy résolut de prendre possession de cette isle [Grenade] [...] mais la multitude des Sauvages qui l'habitoient, et son éloignement de celle de Saint Christophe, luy firent changer de dessein.* (Du Tertre 1667, 425)

> [As far back as 1638, Mr de Poincy decided to take possession of this island [Grenada] [...]. However, the large numbers of Savages who inhabited it and its distance from St. Christopher led him to change his mind.]

The 'Savages' mentioned in this account are the Kalinago people.

In 1649, Jacques Dyel du Parquet, then Governor of Martinique, led an expedition from Martinique to Grenada in a ship laden with such supplies as cassava, brandy and glass beads, as well as ammunition. As

---

[4] Middle French (fourteenth to early seventeenth centuries) — the intermediate linguistic period preceding modern French.

Du Parquet's ultimate goal was to colonise and acquire Grenada, some of these supplies, in addition to providing victuals for his men while at sea, were likely intended to be used to appease or 'trade' with the Kalinago (glass beads) or to provide protection in the event of conflict (ammunition) with these indigenous people, depending on the turn that events took once his party had landed in Grenada. Du Parquet's formal acquisition of Grenada occurred in 1650, when he purchased Grenada and the Grenadines, along with Martinique and St. Lucia, from the Compagnie des Isles d'Amérique for 41,500 *livres tournois* (Tours pounds—one of several currencies used in France during that era)[5] (Roget 1983, 15). It should be noted that when Grenada was 'sold', it had long been the home of the Kalinago people, who clearly saw the island as their own. At the time, there was much money to be made from tobacco production, and these Frenchmen considered Grenada a suitable place to expand production of this crop.

Consensus is lacking among historians on the events that followed. Some say that Du Parquet was well received by the Kalinago when he landed in Grenada and, capitalising on this hospitable reception, quickly proceeded to conclude a treaty with the Kalinago chief (known as Kaïrouane), under which Grenada was partitioned between the French and the Kalinago. The French would inhabit the southern and western part of the island (Basseterre) while the Kalinago would live in the eastern and northern part of the island (Cabesterre) (Steele 2003, 39). The French then proceeded to construct a fortified settlement in Basseterre, known as St. Louis. Other historians dispute the claim that any agreement or treaty was concluded, arguing instead that the Kalinago were duped by the French when the latter offered them assistance with resisting British land-grabbing efforts. In any event, it appears that the Kalinago either were led to believe or simply did believe that the French were in Grenada temporarily, when in fact they had come to stay. Shortly after arriving in Grenada, the French established a large tobacco plantation in the modern-day Tanteen area (Brizan 1984, 17), with the first crop being reaped some months later.

Once the Kalinago realised that the French were in Grenada not as visitors but as settlers, they organised themselves in a bid to drive them

---

[5] A number of sources indicate that the purchase price was 60,000 *livres tournois*.

off the island. Kalinago attacks on the French began less than one year after the settlers had arrived in Grenada. Du Parquet had returned to Martinique after appointing Jean Le Comte as Governor of Grenada. In 1651, faced with ongoing Kalinago opposition, the French, who received assistance from other islands in warding off Kalinago attacks, decided to put an end to Kalinago resistance. Their main mission was to push the Kalinago to the north of the island or to drive them out of Grenada completely. Although the Kalinago fought bravely on the day of the attack, they came under a barrage of fire from the French. They sought refuge in the surrounding woods but the French continued to pursue them doggedly, killing as many as they could. Recounting the actual fighting between the French and Kalinago, Grenadian historian George Brizan states:

> A band of about 40 [Kalinago] pressed further north until they reached the northernmost point of the island, but realising the hopelessness of their situation and, with French soldiers close at hand, the impossibility of escape, covering their eyes with their hands they plunged into the sea to meet what to them was a glorious end, compared to a base and shameful death at the hands of the Frenchman. The French pursuit of the Caribs lasted several days, beginning in St. George (Basseterre) and ending at Le Morne des Sauteurs or Leapers' Hill, the name subsequently given to the spot from which the Caribs plunged. In 1664 the Dominican order of the Catholic Church laid the foundation of a church there. (Brizan 1984, 18-19)

Following this brutal attack, the *Histoire Générale des Antilles Habitées par les François* tells us that:

> *Les François[6] ne perdirent qu'un seul homme dans cette expédition, apres laquelle ils brûlerent toutes les cases, détruisirent les jardins, arracherent le manyoc, enleverent tous ce qu'ils trouverent chez les Sauvages, et s'en retournerent bien joyeux, ne croyant pas que ceux qui estoient échapez fussent*

---

[6] Middle French (fourteenth to early seventeenth centuries)—the intermediate linguistic period preceding modern French.

assez téméraires pour entreprendre un second combat. (Du Tertre 1667, 430)

[The French lost only one man in this mission, after which they burned down all the huts, destroyed the crops, uprooted the manioc plants, and carted off everything they found on the property of the Savages. They were quite jubilant when they returned, as they did not believe that those who had escaped would have the temerity to launch a second attack.]

Le Morne des Sauteurs or Leapers' Hill in Grenada is a hauntingly beautiful place. Located in the north of Grenada, in a windswept spot overlooking the Atlantic Ocean and Caribbean Sea, a view from the precipice from which the Kalinago leapt to their deaths reveals roiling, angry waters that relentlessly pound sharp, jagged rocks. Standing on the edge of this precipice fills one with a profound sense of awe. It is as though one has set foot on hallowed ground that harbours truths that have not been fully told about a people whose history has been recorded from a decidedly Eurocentric perspective. The powerful impact produced by Leapers' Hill is depicted in one of two complementary films entitled *Caribs' Leap* and *Western Deep*, produced by acclaimed British-Grenadian filmmaker Steve McQueen. In *Caribs' Leap*, filmed at Leapers' Hill, McQueen portrays the courageous choice made by the Kalinago to leap to their deaths at this historical landmark rather than surrender to a life of subjugation. Leapers' Hill therefore stands as a stark and enduring symbol of the near annihilation of the Kalinago people and their descendants, wherever they may now live.

Illustration 1.1
The Leapers' Hill (Le Morne des Sauteurs) monument
This marks the spot from which the Kalinago (Caribs) leapt to their deaths rather than face subjugation by the French.

Although the Leapers' Hill event was a seminal one that spelled gloom for the future survival of the Kalinago of Grenada, some remained in the northern part of the island. News of the genocide of Grenada's Kalinago spread to their fellow Kalinago in neighbouring islands, particularly St. Vincent. Enraged, the Kalinago in that island decided to retaliate, launching surprise attacks on the French in Grenada and creating a siege mentality among them, which forced them to remain largely holed up in Basseterre. Particularly effective was what Hilary Beckles describes as a 'strike and sail' strategy, which involved fellow Kalinago entering Grenada by sea, killing or harassing the French and departing swiftly in their boats again.

In 1654, tired of the constant harassment by the Kalinago, Governor Le Comte organised a force of 150 men who travelled to the north of the island and launched a surprise attack on the most heavily populated Kalinago settlement, killing everyone they encountered, regardless of gender or age. The French then proceeded to burn all the homes of the Kalinago and to destroy their boats and canoes. Although skirmishes between the French and Grenada's surviving Kalinago, the latter assisted by their Kalinago brethren in nearby islands, would continue for a few more years, the 1654 scorched earth attack by the French effectively marked the demise of the Kalinago in Grenada.

The Kalinago in the Lesser Antilles resisted European colonising agents for as long as they could. In the end, however, few Kalinago survived their efforts to annihilate them completely. Between 1492 and 1700, the Kalinago population in the Lesser Antilles is estimated to have fallen by as much as 90 percent. Today, Dominica is the only Anglophone island with fairly significant numbers of Kalinago (roughly 3,000). Some 3,700 acres of land have been set aside for this population on the island's east coast. Relatively small numbers of Kalinago descendants remain in St. Vincent. In addition, as mentioned above, the Garinagu or 'Black Caribs' are present along the Caribbean coast of a number of Central American countries, as a result of their mass expulsion from St. Vincent in 1797 by the British. Before being exiled, some 5,000 of these Garinagu were imprisoned on Balliceaux Island off the coast of St. Vincent, where roughly half of them perished before making the forced trip to Central America.

As with the other Caribbean islands they inhabited for hundreds of years before the arrival of the Europeans, the Kalinago have not only contributed to Grenada's culture through their food, pottery and fishing techniques, but have also enriched Grenadian vocabulary with such everyday words as *agouti, manioc, ajoupa* (hut), *boutou, roukou*[7] (a common plant in Grenada and elsewhere used as a dye and a food colourant, also known as *annatto* and *achiote*), *hurricane, boucan* (a wooden structure with trays used for drying cocoa), *titiree* (a tiny freshwater fish or whitebait) and of course *Carriacou*. A number of linguists also believe that the indigenous people influenced the structure of Lesser Antillean French-lexicon Creole through contact occurring in a context of marronage (Africans fleeing slavery and seeking refuge in indigenous communities), particularly in the case of St. Lucia.

Illustration 1.2 The *roukou* plant (*Bixa orellana*)
Roukou is believed to be a Tupi-derived word. The plant's seeds are used as a dye and as a natural food colourant in dishes in Grenada, including the island's national dish, oil down.

---

[7] The word *roukou* is thought to have a Tupi origin. The Tupi are Brazilian indigenous people, generally believed to have first settled in the Amazon rainforest before migrating to other regions.

2

COLONISATION, ENSLAVEMENT AND THE RISE AND FALL OF THE KÉYÒL LANGUAGE

Central to any study of Lesser Antillean French-lexicon Creole is the presence of French colonisers and enslaved Africans in the Lesser Antilles, as this language came into being as a result of contact between these two groups. As the presence of Africans in Grenada is discussed below, the focus here is on the establishment of French colonies in the Caribbean generally and specifically in Grenada.

The first French colony in the Caribbean was established in St. Kitts in 1625. The French were not, however, the only settlers there: the British had arrived two years earlier, and the island was partitioned between these two colonising forces. The relationship between the British and the French on St. Kitts was tense, and the island was the scene of persistent rivalries and fighting between the two colonial forces for roughly 85 years, until it officially became a British possession in 1713 under the Treaty of Utrecht. Although it is believed that the first seeds of the French-lexicon Creole language were planted on St. Kitts, there is currently little or no trace of it there.

From St. Kitts, French colonisers managed to gain control of Martinique and Guadeloupe, countries where Lesser Antillean French-lexicon Creole is spoken today, alongside French, the official language. Haiti and its French-lexicon Creole language deserve special mention. The French presence in Haiti, a Greater Antillean country, became official in 1697 when the Treaty of Rijswijk was concluded. Under the terms of this treaty, the western portion of Hispaniola, which would be named Saint Domingue and later Haiti, was ceded to France. Haiti's history differs in two important and significant ways from that of the Lesser Antillean islands. First, a relatively large number of Africans (approximately

800,000) were taken to work on the plantations of Haiti, once known as the Pearl of the Antilles. Second, Haiti became the first black republic in 1804, after a massive and successful revolt by the enslaved led to the expulsion of the French. However, this victory cost Haiti dearly, as France, Britain and the United States imposed an embargo on it that ravaged its economy for a protracted period. Compounding Haiti's financial woes after it became a republic was France's demand for compensation to the tune of 150 million gold francs, later reduced to 90 million, for 'lost' property, a reference that includes the 'loss' of its labour force, which remained on the island after France's expulsion. It therefore stands to reason that Haiti's French-lexicon Creole (Kreyòl) would be somewhat different from Lesser Antillean French-lexicon Creole. Nonetheless, the areas of overlap between these two French-lexicon Creole varieties are significant, as they belong to one family of languages.

From the islands of Martinique and Guadeloupe, the French proceeded to expand their colonies to include the nearby islands of St. Lucia, Dominica and Grenada; the French settlement of Grenada in 1649 and their swift decimation of the Kalinago people which ensued are described above.

Although published works on Grenada's early history are generally scant, two works provide fairly extensive information on the settlement of the French in Grenada. The first is a manuscript entitled *Histoire de l'Isle de Grenade en Amérique: 1649-1659* [History of the Island of Grenada in the Americas: 1649-1659]. Interestingly, this document was written by an individual who preferred to remain in the shadows and signed his name simply as *'Anonyme'* (Anonymous). The frequent religious references in this manuscript suggest that it was probably written by a priest or clergyman. Jacques Petitjean Roget, who wrote an introduction to the book, attributes the manuscript to Bénigne Bresson, a Dominican missionary who travelled from Dieppe (in the Upper Normandy region of France) to the Caribbean and lived in Grenada for a few years. The second is Du Tertre's four-volume *Histoire Générale des Antilles Habitées par les François*.

In addition to the obstacles to colonisation that the Kalinago presented as described above, the French had to contend with trouble within their own ranks. Jean Le Comte, the Governor of Grenada appointed by Du Parquet, drowned in 1654 as he and others departed the scene of the Kalinago attack in the north of the island by boat. Upon Le Comte's death, a man named Le Fort sought to become Governor, while Louis de Cacqueray de Valmenière was also laying claim to this title. Du Tertre states, with respect to these competing claims for the position of Governor, that *'toute l'Isle se trouv[ait] pour lors dans une épouvantable division'* (Du Tertre 1667, 432) ['the whole island was in a frightful state of division']. As a result, some 100 soldiers were rounded up and sent to help restore order in Grenada; Cacqueray de Valmenière ultimately prevailed. In the end, however, as Du Tertre states with reference to Grenada, *'cette colonie a épuisé la meilleure partie de son bien'* (Du Tertre 1667, 433) ['this colony depleted most of his (Cacqueray de Valmenière's) assets'].

Having purchased Grenada in 1650, Du Parquet sold Grenada to the Comte de Cérrillac in 1657 due to the financial problems created mainly by constant conflict with the Kalinago. King Louis XIV then went on to purchase the island in 1664, placing it in the hands of the French West India Company. Finally, with the dissolution of the French West India Company in 1674, Grenada fell under the direct control of the French Crown, thus becoming a French colony. Grenada would be under some form of uninterrupted French control for 114 years—from 1649 to 1763.

As promising an island as Grenada was to colonising agents owing to its geographic location and various other attributes, the island nonetheless proved, at various points, to be more of a liability than an asset because it was so often the scene of unrest. So it was in bygone eras, and so it is today: tiny Grenada has long been a theatre of simmering tensions stoked by political and other factors that sporadically erupt, sometimes quite unpredictably, into conflict, violence and bloodshed.

While under French control, Grenada was divided into the following six parishes: Basseterre (St. George's), Ance Goyave (St. John's), Grand Pauvre (St. Mark's), Sauteurs (St. Patrick's), Grand Marquis (St. Andrew's) and Maigrin (St. David's).

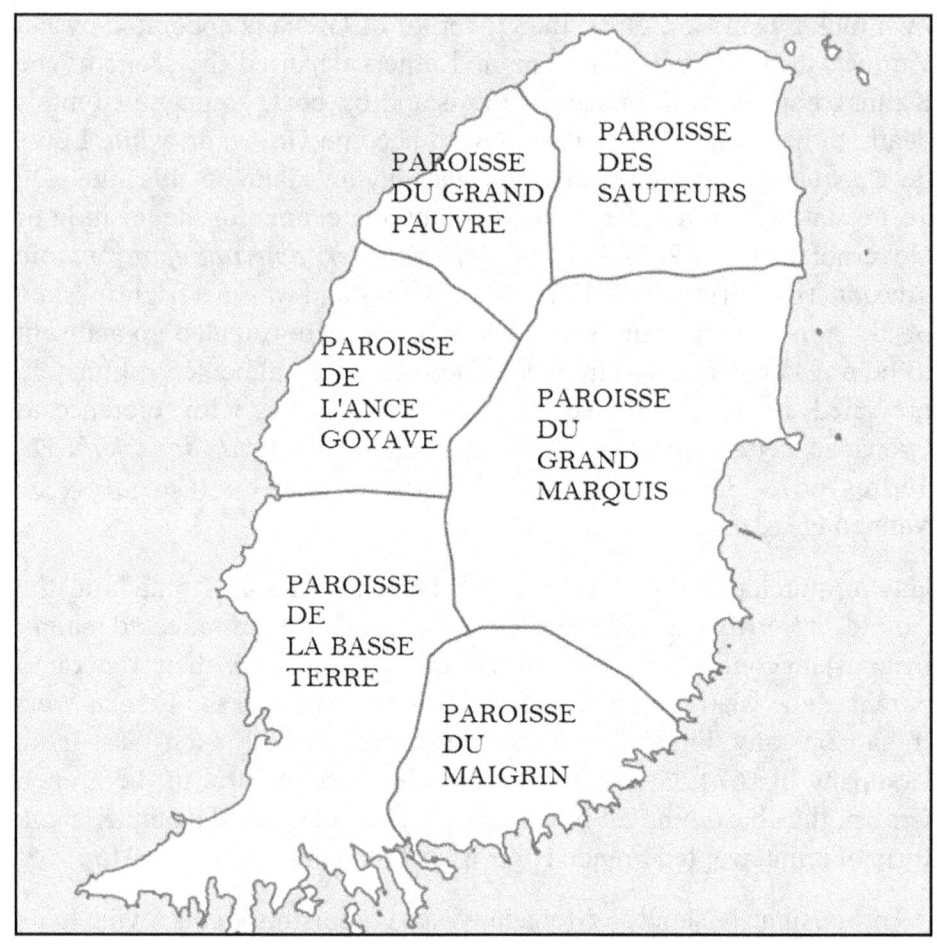

Illustration 2.1 Map of the parishes of Grenada
This map shows the French names used
during the era of French colonisation.

The name 'Paroisse de l'Anse Goyave' reveals the origin of the modern-day area known as the 'Lance' in Gouyave. The British merely overlaid these French parish names with the English ones we know today; the majority of other French place names in Grenada were left virtually intact (see toponyms on page 58).

French control of Grenada ended in 1763, when the British took possession of the island under the Treaty of Paris. However, for an additional four-year period, from 1779 to 1783, Grenada once again came under French rule. Britain then regained control of the island under the Treaty of Versailles on 3 September 1783 and it remained a British colony until it became independent in 1974. For the purpose of this study of Grenada's French-lexicon Creole, the unbroken 114-year period of French rule and African presence in Grenada are undoubtedly the most significant factors in the genesis and development of the island's Kéyòl.

Kéyòl, Kwéyòl or Patois?

Before exploring the origins of Grenada's Kéyòl language, further discussion of my choice of the term Kéyòl is in order, given the plethora of terms used to refer to this language: 'French Creole', 'Creole French', 'French-lexicon Creole', 'Créole', 'Creole', 'Kwéyòl', 'Kréyol', 'Kreyòl', 'Kéyòl', 'Kheuol', 'Patúa', 'Patuá', 'Patwa' and 'Patois'.

The term 'Patois' continues to be used in Grenada and Trinidad & Tobago to refer to the French-lexicon Creole of these islands. However, as indicated in the preface, I decided against using the word 'Patois' in this book and opted for 'Kéyòl' instead. I did so because of what I consider to be the biased views that lie behind the definition of the word 'Patois' in the historical contexts of the enslavement and oppression of a people of African ancestry. The irony of using a highly charged negative word such as 'Patois' in a book that seeks to elevate and preserve the language would, in fact, be nothing short of bitter. The Lesser Antillean Anglophone islands of St. Lucia and Dominica, whose history is in many respects similar to Grenada's, have, over the years, transitioned from using the word 'Patois' in their everyday discourse to adopting the word 'Kwéyòl'.

The secondary or extended definition of the word 'patois' appearing in the *Petit Robert* French dictionary is provided in the preface. A more complete (or primary) definition of the word taken from that dictionary appears below:

> *Dialecte local employé par une population généralement peu nombreuse, souvent rurale et dont la culture, le niveau de civilisation sont inférieurs à ceux du milieu environnant.* (Robert 1807)

> [Local dialect spoken by a generally small group of people, often living in rural areas, whose level of education and cultural development are inferior to those of the surrounding milieu.]

This definition speaks for itself.

The meaning of the word 'creole' has evolved over time. David DeCamp provides Dell Hymes's description of the historical evolution of the term:

> The term 'creole' (from Portuguese *crioulo*, via Spanish and French) originally meant a white man of European descent born and raised in a tropical colony. Only later was the meaning extended to include the indigenous natives and others of non-European origin, e.g., African slaves. The term was then applied to certain languages spoken by creoles in and around the Caribbean and in West Africa, and was later extended to other languages of similar types. Most creoles ... are European based, i.e., each has derived most of its vocabulary from one or more European languages. Creole French (also called patois) and Creole English are the most frequent in West Africa and the New World. (DeCamp 1968, 31)

In many islands of the Caribbean and even outside this region, the word 'creole', when used in a linguistic context, therefore refers to the languages born of interaction between the languages of Europeans and Africans. In the case of French-lexicon Creole, the term 'Créole' ('Kreyòl' in Haiti, 'Kwéyòl' in St. Lucia and Dominica, 'Créole' in Martinique and Guadeloupe and 'Kéyòl' in Grenada) refers to the language derived from contact between a number of African languages and the French language.

Grenada's French-lexicon Creole fits the context described above. Perhaps the time has come for modern-day Grenada to consider replacing the word 'Patois' with the word 'Kéyòl' in the island's lexicon, as the latter term more aptly describes this language and bestows on it the dignity it deserves.

The Origins of Grenada's Kéyòl

No specific date can be ascribed to the birth of Lesser Antillean French-lexicon Creole. The development of a language is a dynamic process rather than an event. Roughly speaking, the language as we know it today appears to have developed between the late 1600s and early 1700s.

The Atlantic slave trade, the largest forced migration in recorded history, brought around 10–15 million Africans to the Americas, with more than 40 percent being brought to the Caribbean. In an article entitled 'Africa and the Caribbean: Overview', Denis Hidalgo states:

> Slave traders bound for the Caribbean took about 80 percent of their captives from a vast coastline that stretched for 3,500 miles [5,600 km] along the West and Central African coast. In modern terms, this began with the nation of Senegal in the north to Angola in the south. It also penetrated into the African interior, between 500 and 1,000 miles [800 to 1,600 km]. About 20 percent overall came from the region of Mozambique in south-east Africa. (Hidalgo 2012, 4-5)

However, little is known about the precise regions from which Grenada's African population came and thus of its linguistic origins. In his book *Grenada, Island of Conflict*, Grenadian historian George Brizan (1984, 86) states:

> Grenada shared in both French and British slave imports. It is estimated that between 1650 and 1808 the British West Indies received 1.9 million slaves and between 1664 and 1830 the French colonies received 1.6 million slaves. Figures on Grenada's slave imports are very fragmentary: she received 1,594 in 1763; 9,752 in the period 1784–1787; 2,190 in 1802–1803.

In *From Columbus to Castro: The History of the Caribbean*, Eric Williams (1970) notes that the ratio of whites to blacks in Grenada changed from 1:2 in the year 1700 (251 whites to 525 blacks) to 1:25 in the year 1783 (996 whites to 24,620 blacks).

It is also known that the French had trading posts in St Louis, at the mouth of the Senegal River, and established posts in Gorée (near modern-day Dakar), in Assini, near modern-day Abidjan in Côte d'Ivoire, and at modern-day Ouidah, in Benin, formerly Dahomey in the latter part of the 1600s. A museum has been built on the island of Gorée, off the coast of Senegal, very near Dakar, memorialising the Atlantic slave trade. This island's slave quarters and its Door of No Return, which face the Atlantic Ocean, stand as a powerful reminder of one of the ugliest chapters in modern human history, the effects of which continue to be felt in myriad ways to this day.

Africans were brought to Grenada in the late 1600s, throughout the 1700s, and in the early 1800s to supply the manual labour needed on the island's plantations. Some of these Africans may have come directly from West Africa, while others are thought to have come to Grenada via Martinique.

However, into the dark void of information on the precise African origins of most modern-day Grenadians shines one ray of light: an analysis carried out by Frances Kay Brinkley of a 1750 census of Carriacou (Brinkley 1978). This census is housed in France's National Archives. The Brinkley document indicates that the Commandant of Carriacou, Mr de la Bourgerie du Sablon, was given instructions to conduct this census. Based on this handwritten document, there were roughly 200 people (or 'souls', as they were called) living in Carriacou in 1750. Of persons in the 15–50 age group, 53 were white, 33 were black (and, for the most part, enslaved) and three were designated as mulatto. The fascinating aspect of the census is that it lists the first names of a number of the Africans or blacks in Carriacou at the time, followed by the name of their ethnic groups, with no last names being provided. For example, in the Quartier de la Baye des Juifs (the modern-day Limlair-Tibeau area), there is a listing of 'Angélique Negresse Ibo' [Angélique, Ibo black woman] and 'Antoine Congo'. Overall, this census identifies eight persons as Congo, three as Bambara, one as 'Mandong' (a likely misspelling of the word Mende, an ethnic group in Sierra Leone), two as Ibo, three as Arada (a town in Eastern Chad), two as 'Aura' (a possible misspelled reference to the Ora people of Nigeria) and one as 'Anan' (a likely misspelling of the Anaang people of south-eastern Nigeria).

Culturally rich Carriacou provides further insight into the regions of West Africa from which Grenada's black population came in a number of the songs that accompany the African-derived Big Drum Dance rituals on this island. A number of these songs are sung in Kéyòl and some contain words, such as *Dahomey*, *Cromanti*, *Congo* and *Temne*, that may help a researcher ascertain with some precision the region or countries of origin of the Africans who were brought to Grenada's shores. An additional indication of the origins of Grenada's present-day population can be found in the religious practices and folk tales that are still very much alive on the island, such as *Obeah* in the case of the former and Anansi stories in the case of the latter. One clear link between Grenada and West Africa is the practice of Shango (*Xangô*) on the island, discussed in greater detail later on. Research has revealed that the songs sung at Shango ceremonies in Grenada are of Yoruba origin. Lastly, some words used in Grenada are borrowed from West African languages. These include *béké* ('white person') < Igbo *beké*; *boli* 'calabash' < Soninke, Wolof *boli*; *congori* 'millipede' < Bangi *ngongoli*, among other West African languages; *jouk* 'prick' < Fulani *jukka*; *jumbie* 'evil spirit' < Kikongo *nzáambi*, Kimbundu *nzumbi*; *Obeah* 'use of supernatural forces to protect or inflict harm on the living', possibly < Twi *obayifo*; and *sousou* 'pooled savings' < Yoruba *Èsúsú*.[8]

Illustration 2.2 A *boli* (calabash) tree (*Crescentia cujete*)
Boli is a loan word from a number of West African languages.

As indicated earlier, Grenadian Kéyòl, as a contact language, has drawn most of its vocabulary from French and its syntax from African

---

[8] The African origin of all terms was obtained from Winer (2009), with the exception of the terms *boli* and *jumbie*. The definition of *boli* was obtained from Diagana (2013), while the etymologies for *jumbie* were taken from Laman (1964) for Kikongo and da Silva (1964) for Kimbundu.

languages. Perhaps this is what Aimé Césaire, the famous Martiniquan poet and writer, had in mind when he said that 'the body of the Creole language is French, but its soul is African'. Similarly, in his book *Caribbean and African Languages: Social History, Language, Literature and Education*, Morgan Dalphinis (1985, 95) states:

> Both in an analysis of the Creole languages of the Caribbean as well as Caribbean culture, it is clear that Europe has affected Africa but equally Africa has affected Europe: the words are European, but the syntax is African.

This study is limited to an exploration of the lexical aspect of Grenadian Kéyòl, that is, the French words or vocabulary from which the lexicon of Grenada's Kéyòl language is derived.

Grenada's Kéyòl belongs to a sub-group of French-lexicon Creole known as Lesser Antillean French-lexicon Creole. The Lesser Antilles is subdivided into the Leeward Islands and Windward Islands. Lesser Antillean French-lexicon Creole is still spoken by a few persons in Grenada and to varying degrees in Trinidad, Venezuela, St. Lucia, Dominica, Martinique and Guadeloupe. In terms of Anglophone islands, French-lexicon Creole is very much alive in Dominica and St. Lucia, while it is on the verge of extinction in Grenada and Trinidad. (See video **Chapter 6: Social Dimensions of Kéyòl**; *Lesser Antillean French-lexicon Creole* video clip.) The reasons for the divergent paths taken by this language over the years will be examined later. While there may be minor variations in the French-lexicon Creole language from one Lesser Antillean country to the next, the speakers from these islands are able to communicate with each other with great ease. Modern-day Lesser Antillean French-lexicon Creole appears to have stabilised in its present form in the early eighteenth century. A visitor to Martinique in 1701 is reported to have heard a woman of African ancestry accuse a man of being the father of her child by stating: '*Toi papa li*' [you are its father], a sentence that bears similarity to modern-day French-lexicon Creole. (Holm 1989, 365)

In Grenada, during the period of slavery, and particularly during the period when the French controlled the island, the plantation system was the incubator for the development and stabilisation of Kéyòl as a language of communication. This system and the factors that influenced the development of Kéyòl are not unique to Grenada: the development of French-lexicon Creole in other islands was influenced by a similar set of circumstances and factors, bearing in mind the common features shared by French-lexicon Creole in general and the ability of its speakers, even beyond the Lesser Antillean language subgroup, to communicate with each other, albeit to varying degrees. African people, uprooted from different parts of the African continent and brought to the plantations to toil in brutal and inhumane conditions, had no common unifying language and thus found themselves in a situation where they had to communicate not only among themselves but also with European colonising agents. The practice of some enslavers of deliberately placing Africans who spoke a common African language on different plantations in order to minimise the chances of rebellion and insurrection may also have had the effect of fairly quickly solidifying French-lexicon Creole as the language of communication among the workforce. In Grenada, as in many other islands, Kéyòl emerged as the *lingua franca* of Africans in the New World to communicate among themselves and with French colonising forces.

The Rise and Fall of the Kéyòl Language in Grenada

For roughly 100 years, from the early 1700s to the early 1800s, virtually everyone in Grenada spoke Kéyòl, with many people, particularly in the lower socio-economic groups, being monolingual Kéyòl speakers. Although English started to supplant Kéyòl in the 1800s, the language was widely spoken in Grenada until the 1930s. A census conducted in 1783, the year the British took control of Grenada, indicates that in a population of 30,371, only 690 (two percent) spoke Standard English or some recognisable form of English. Indeed, official documents were being issued in French in Grenada well into the 1800s. One factor that would have worked in favour of the development and maturation of Kéyòl in Grenada is the island's size. Grenada is a small island and it is logical to assume that this would have led to greater contact and interaction both among the enslaved and between the enslaved and the enslavers.

While it must be borne in mind that the European colonising agents, whether French or British, had one common aim—to use African labour in order to amass wealth—there seems to be a feeling that the French treated this workforce in a more humane manner than the British. This view is not universally shared, however. In his doctoral thesis *The Economic Aspect of the Abolition of the West Indian Slave Trade and Slavery*, Eric Williams (1938), a distinguished Trinidadian scholar, historian and politician and the island's first Prime Minister, argues:

> There was no fundamental difference between the French and the British slave owner: in both cases it is not individuals we have to deal with but the hard inescapable logic of economic necessity. (p. 46)

The French *Code Noir*, a decree passed by France's King Louis XIV in 1685, essentially codified the separation between masters and the enslaved and gave the former much latitude in punishing the latter. In general terms, however, the view that the French treated enslaved Africans in somewhat less barbaric ways than the British seems credible. In addition, France, unlike Britain, has historically had an assimilationist policy, which may have led to somewhat less inhumane treatment of its African workforce, despite the fact that this policy was ultimately intended to solidify and promote the interests of France. In 1700, Jean-Baptiste Labat, a French missionary from the Dominican order, wrote the following, after seeing how slaves in Barbados were treated: 'The English do not look after their slaves well, and feed them very badly ... the overseers get every ounce of work out of them, beat them without mercy for the least fault, and appear to care less for the life of a negro than for a horse'.

This is corroborated by events in Grenada. In reference to the takeover of Grenada by the British, French Jesuit priest Guillaume-Thomas François Raynal wrote in his book, *A Philosophical and Political History of the Settlements and Trade of the Europeans in the East and West Indies*, first published in 1770:

> The new proprietors, blinded no doubt by national pride, have substituted new methods to those of their predecessors. They chose to alter the way of the slaves. The negroes, who, from their very ignorance are more attached to their old customs than other men, have revolted ... the whole colony was filled with suspicion.

This comment is significant for two reasons: first, the reference to the 'ignorance' of the 'negroes' reveals the deep-seated prejudice towards people of African ancestry in Grenada at the time, regardless of the colonising agent, and second, it appears to corroborate the preference of Grenadians of that era for the French way of life. The latter is one of the factors that may have played a role in sowing the seeds of the rebellion led by Julien Fédon, a free coloured of French descent, who is widely viewed as a hero in Grenada's history. Indeed, the position taken by most black Grenadians during the Fédon rebellion makes it clear that this group, which accounted for the majority of the Grenadian population, felt greater affinity to the French and the French language and backed the French in hostilities with the British.

Beginning in the 1930s, Kéyòl began to disappear as the language of communication in Grenada and to be rapidly replaced by English. Of course, the language did not disappear overnight, but the speed with which it lost ground to English is remarkable. By the 1950s, while many people could still understand Kéyòl, the number who could hold a sustained conversation in it had fallen precipitously. By the 1970s, Kéyòl speakers were limited to a tiny minority of elderly people living in rural areas. Today, in 2016, the handful of people who can speak the language fluently have three things in common: they were raised by their grandmothers and were fortunate enough to speak Kéyòl with them, they live in the rural areas of Grenada, and they are elderly (in their 70s and 80s). (See video **Chapter 6: Social Dimensions of Kéyòl**; *Grandparents as the Vehicle for Language Transmission* video clip.) Sadly, when these people die, the Kéyòl language in Grenada will disappear with them. In St. Lucia and Dominica, the situation is quite different: French-lexicon Creole has survived in these islands and, to some degree, can be said to be currently thriving, as many young people now view the language as a source of national pride and identity. St. Lucia celebrates a *Jounen Kwéyòl* (Creole Day), while in Dominica, the Kwéyòl words *'Apres Bondie C'est La Ter'* ('After God, the land') are emblazoned on the island's coat of arms. Why did French-lexicon Creole, which emerged in St. Lucia and Dominica at roughly the same period as it did in Grenada, die out so quickly in Grenada to the point where it is now on the verge of becoming a lost language, while this same language is currently very much alive and mostly well in St. Lucia and Dominica? This will be discussed in detail below.

Separate mention must be made of Trinidad's linguistic history, as Grenada exerted a significant influence in this area. The linguistic history of Trinidad, which bears a number of close parallels to Grenada's own linguistic history, is nonetheless unique in that although the island was never colonised by the French, French-lexicon Creole was widely spoken on the island from the end of the eighteenth century to the end of the nineteenth century. This is explained by the fact that while the island was in the hands of the Spanish, it was underpopulated and neglected. To boost the population, the Spanish authorities issued an edict in 1783 called the *Cédula de Población* (a less successful *Cédula* had been issued in 1776), which completely altered the linguistic landscape of the island. A French planter from Grenada played an instrumental role in this second *Cédula*. Philippe-Rose Roume de Saint-Laurent had visited Trinidad earlier and was very impressed with the island's potential. He wrote a report urging that incentives be granted to colonists from the French and former French islands to encourage them to migrate to Trinidad. This edict provided land grants to Roman Catholic settlers from other islands and their workforce. In addition to the more generous terms of this second *Cédula*, one of the reasons for its success was the unrest being experienced in the French-owned Caribbean islands as a consequence of the French Revolution (1789-1799). Referring to the *Cédula*, Elodie Jourdain, a Martiniquan and one of the first persons to document that island's French-lexicon Creole, stated in her book *Du français aux parlers créoles*:

> *[Les Espagnols] firent donc appel à nos colons en leur offrant de solides avantages. Ceux-ci exigèrent avant tout deux choses: l'emploi officiel de la langue française, au même titre que la castillane et la conservation garantie de la qualité de Français, non seulement pour eux, mais pour leurs descendants. L'Espagne acquiesça à toutes leurs demandes, et une nouvelle émigration eut lieu des Antilles françaises, surtout de la Grenade vers la Trinidad.* (Jourdain 1956, xvi)

[[The Spanish] thus extended an invitation to our settlers by offering them substantial benefits. The latter made two main demands: the official use of the French language, on an equal footing with Spanish, and the guarantee that the French identity would be preserved not only for them, but also for their descendants. Spain acceded to all their demands, and a new wave of immigration took place from the French West Indies, particularly from Grenada to Trinidad.]

Trinidad's linguistic history was therefore heavily influenced by events in Grenada and the ties between the two islands have historically been close; a great deal of contact continues even to the present. With the influx of immigrants from the French-speaking islands in the late 1700s, French-lexicon Creole soon became Trinidad's *lingua franca*. The island's French-lexicon Creole language has followed a trajectory similar to Grenada's: it is very much endangered and is spoken in only a few small communities of the island, such as Blanchisseuse, Moruga, Paramin and San Raphael. However, Trinidad may be one step ahead of Grenada in that active efforts are being made by a dedicated few to preserve and even revive the language by documenting it, recording its speakers and teaching it so that it can be passed on to future generations.

Returning to Grenada's Kéyòl, it is therefore with a mixture of joy and sadness that I spoke to and arranged for interviews with the island's remaining Kéyòl speakers, featured in the video that constitutes the third part of this work. My joy comes from listening to the sound of this beautiful language, the first language of the descendants of Africans who were forcibly brought to Grenada's shores. As one of Grenada's Kéyòl speakers said to me: 'we are not English men, we are not Americans; we are Grenadians ... Patois is a nice language'. (See video **Chapter 6: Social Dimensions of Kéyòl**; *Pride in the Kéyòl Language* video clip.) While some efforts are being made in Grenada to preserve the Kéyòl language in the cultural sphere and the vines of this language remain firmly and intricately intertwined with Grenadian English-lexicon Creole, my feelings of sadness are rooted in the realisation that as a language of everyday communication, Kéyòl teeters on the brink of extinction in Grenada.

Factors behind the Decline of the Kéyòl Language in Grenada

A confluence of factors accounts for the decline of Grenada's Kéyòl and the fact that this language, which during the 1800s was the *lingua franca* of the islands of St. Lucia, Dominica, Trinidad and Grenada (all of which are Anglophone islands today), has survived in St. Lucia and Dominica but is verging on complete disappearance in Grenada in 2016. In fact, Dominica, Grenada and St. Lucia share much in common historically: these islands went back and forth between the British and the French as colonial rivalries played out; they then became British colonies between the late 1700s and early 1800s until the time of their independence in the 1970s.

Geography

In the chain of Caribbean islands, Dominica lies between Martinique and Guadeloupe, both French-speaking islands (officially Overseas Departments of France), where the same French-lexicon Creole is spoken. Dominica's geographic proximity to these two French-speaking islands naturally leads to extensive linguistic contact with them. Currently, there are ferries that travel regularly between Dominica, Martinique, Guadeloupe and St. Lucia, facilitating constant interaction among the people of these islands. It therefore stands to reason that Dominica's proximity to and contact with Martinique and Guadeloupe would serve as a major factor in the preservation of the island's Kwéyòl.

In the case of St. Lucia also, geography has been critical to the preservation of Kwéyòl. St. Lucia is roughly 25 miles from Martinique (measured from the northern tip of St. Lucia to the southern tip of Martinique). As noted above, St. Lucia is included in the ferry service that travels to Martinique and Guadeloupe several times a week and there is a great deal of movement between the two islands. It is not uncommon, for example, for someone who needs a car part in St. Lucia to travel to Martinique to obtain it. Once again, frequent and ongoing contact with French- and French-lexicon-Creole-speaking Martinique has had a very favourable impact on the preservation of Kwéyòl in St. Lucia.

Although unrelated to geography, it should also be noted that, in a cupid-like rivalry, St. Lucia changed hands between France and Britain no fewer than 14 times. Moreover, St. Lucia became a British colony later than Grenada did—in 1814. As late as 1958, it was estimated that only 35 percent of the population could speak English fluently as a second language; 98 percent spoke Kwéyòl as their first language. From a linguistic standpoint, this additional 30-year period of French colonisation of St. Lucia relative to Grenada is another significant factor in the preservation of Kwéyòl in the former.

Compared to the Anglophone islands of Dominica and St. Lucia, Grenada, which lies further away from Martinique and Guadeloupe in the chain of islands, is relatively isolated. The reality is that for quite some time, there has been very little contact between Grenada and these French-speaking islands. Grenada's ties, as mentioned earlier, have historically been with Trinidad, and the trajectory of this language has been the same in both islands: French-lexicon Creole is slipping from their grasp and could, in the not-too-distant future, plunge into the abyss of lost languages.

Geography has therefore played a major role in the decline of Kéyòl in Grenada.

Social Attitudes

A language and its speakers are often viewed through the same lens or prism. If a people are seen as inferior, so is their language. Grenada's Kéyòl was born in the context of slavery and Kéyòl is the language of the enslaved. European slave owners perpetuated the myth of the innate inferiority of Africans for a very long time and the psychological scars of these attitudes are still evident today. They stripped Africans of their humanity, portraying them as savages who came from a distant land bereft of language and culture. Small wonder, therefore, that French-lexicon Creole, the language of the black population, was portrayed as inferior. This language was usually described by Europeans in the most pejorative terms—as the 'baby' talk of the enslaved, as Africans' faulty imitations of their masters' language, as gibberish, as a 'corruption' of the French language and as grammarless, 'broken' French. The fact that French-lexicon Creole is largely an oral language and that efforts to codify its writing system are, for the most part, a recent phenomenon have contributed to the lack of regard for the language.

Indeed, the attitude of the colonial powers to Creole languages, regardless of lexicon or country, generally ranged from dismissive to disparaging to downright bigoted. Take, for example, the statement made by L. J. Leopold, Principal of the Educational Institute in Sierra Leone, in reference to the English-lexicon Krio language:

> The Sierra Leone patois is a kind of invertebrate *omnium gatherum* of all sorts, a veritable *ola* (sic) *podrida* collected from many different languages without regard to harmony or precision: it is largely defective and sadly wanting in many of the essentials and details that make up and dignify a language. It is a standing menace and a disgrace. (Spitzer 1966, 41)

There is no small irony in the attitudes and perceptions of the colonial powers. During the Middle Ages, the languages of the scholarly and erudite in Europe were Greek and Latin. It may come as a surprise to the reader to learn that during this period, French was considered a lowly language, and one looked down upon by society's scholars and thinkers. As late as 1529, in a publication entitled *Declamatio de pueris statim ac liberaliter instituendis* [Declaration on the Subject of Early Liberal Education for Children], Erasmus argued that the French language was 'barbarous and irregular', that 'its spelling does not agree with pronunciation' and that the French language had 'harsh sounds and accents that hardly fall within the realm of human speech' (as cited in Melzer 2012: 62).

The aversion expressed by Erasmus in the 1500s to the French language is remarkably similar to the denigrating language that would be used to describe the French-lexicon Creole language a few hundred years later.

In 1826, the First Annual Report of the Grenada District Committee of the Society for Promoting Christian Knowledge stated, with reference to efforts to communicate with Grenadians:

> It is scarcely possible without an Interpreter, to communicate in their broken and corrupted French, the plain, wholesome, and practical Truths of Christianity. (As cited in Roberts 1997, 216)

Peter Roberts, a Barbadian academician whose 1971 Master's thesis was entitled *The Verb in Grenadian French Creole* and who is one of the very few who have studied Grenada's Kéyòl, described attitudes to Kéyòl in Grenada during that period thus:

> On being asked whether she could speak patois, a lady, now living in St. George's, was rather indignant and felt herself insulted. If there is not always this kind of strong reaction, there may be a more subtle one, when people laugh in an embarrassed manner when asked about patois. This kind of reaction is indicative of insecurity and shame about a past which the person considers to have been backward and unenlightened. When a person is in a serious mood, he or she is usually unwilling to admit that such a past existed and is always too willing to forget it completely. (Roberts 1971, 34)

In 2013 and 2014, in discussions with Grenada's remaining speakers of Kéyòl, most confirmed that the Kéyòl language was once the object of scorn and shame. One elderly woman told me that at the time when it was most widely spoken, Kéyòl was considered to be 'nothing'. Another told me that when her elderly monolingual grandmother spoke to her grandchildren in Kéyòl, they refused to answer in this language, choosing to speak English instead. In these very recent discussions, however, there was no hint of shame, only a palpable sense of nostalgia. During the course of this research, Kéyòl speakers clearly took pride in teaching me everything they could about the Kéyòl language, just as I enjoyed learning about it.

In essence, therefore, because of the scorn heaped on Kéyòl, its speakers in Grenada saw it as a language that was worthless and made no effort to pass it on to their children. Who could blame them? If the attitude to Kéyòl was so negative, if the language was often a source of ridicule, if it was made out to be a corrupted tongue spoken by an inferior people, if it was perceived as hindering rather than helping the advancement and upward mobility of children, why pass it on? English was the language of prestige, the language of upward mobility, while the Kéyòl language was associated with a host of negative conditions—poverty, illiteracy and low socio-economic status.

For Grenadian adults, however, Kéyòl served one very useful purpose: it was used as a language of exclusion for most of the 1900s. Virtually every Grenadian who was exposed to Kéyòl during that period will point to the fact that it was used as a code language, as a means of carrying on an adult conversation in a language that could not be understood by children, since the prevailing attitude in Grenada, then and now, is that children should not be privy to the information or matters discussed by adults. One elderly woman whom I interviewed told me that Kéyòl served its purpose as a language of exclusion because 'children have no right in big people business'. (See video **Chapter 6: Social Dimensions of Kéyòl**; *Kéyòl in the Context of Social and Parental Roles* video clip.)

Because Kéyòl speakers did not feel a sense of pride in their ability to speak the language and did not see the language as having value, they failed to pass it on to future generations, a factor that has greatly contributed to the sharp decline in the number of Kéyòl speakers in Grenada. Social attitudes towards Kéyòl have therefore worked against the preservation of this language.

Education

When the British gained control of Grenada in 1783, the vast majority of Grenada's population would have been illiterate monolingual Kéyòl speakers. During that period, education of the black population was certainly not a priority; in fact, it would perhaps have been perceived more as a threat than a desirable goal.

Later, initial efforts to educate the Grenadian population focused on religious education. For a long time after the British took possession of Grenada, French priests remained on the island. In *The Verb in Grenadian French Creole*, Roberts states the following:

> When the English-speaking priests came eventually and tried to teach the children, they found that patois posed a serious threat, even though as early as 1882 the Board of Education had passed a by-law which stipulated that the use of patois in schools was to be discouraged.

It is therefore obvious that the policy of the British was to minimise, if not eliminate, the use of Kéyòl in schools, and so the language was under attack in both the social and educational spheres. Over time, the transition from European teachers to Grenadian and Barbadian ones ironically led to an even more hostile, anti-Kéyòl stance. Roberts states that with the shift to local teachers, 'French Creole was then more vigorously suppressed, because in addition to the stigma attached to French Creole, it was thought that the speaking of this language prevented the children from learning English'. (Roberts 1971, 29) Added to this was the presence of teachers and headmasters 'from Barbados and other non-French Creole speaking territories and they were hostile towards French Creole' (Roberts 1971, 30).

All the elderly individuals interviewed for this project confirmed that Kéyòl was not spoken in classrooms, even though it may have been used on playgrounds, when teachers were out of earshot. The message conveyed to children in schools was unambiguous: Kéyòl was a language to be ignored, avoided and forgotten.

How could Kéyòl survive when it was being suppressed and degraded in the very schools that were responsible for shaping the thinking and moulding the minds of future leaders?

Religion and Colonial Rivalry

In Grenada, religion served to some degree as a proxy for the expression of fierce colonial rivalries and resentment. The French presence in Grenada spanned the years from 1649 to 1763, after which it changed hands between the British and French for relatively short periods that did not allow sufficient time for wrongs to be righted and festering wounds to heal. After more than one century of unbroken French rule, the British gained control of Grenada from 1763 to 1779, the French from 1779 to 1783 and the British again from 1783 to the time of the island's independence in 1974.

When the British first gained control of the island in 1763 under the Treaty of Paris, the Kéyòl-speaking population of Grenada would have been very much used to the habits and way of life of the French, including their religion, given the relatively large number of French Catholic priests living in Grenada at that time. There is evidence to suggest that in addition to speaking French, some of the priests, who exerted great influence over the population, spoke Kéyòl. Referring to the French priests in Grenada and their relationship with the British, Father Raymund Devas, a British Catholic priest who spent most of his life in Grenada and documented the island's history, notes, 'Who would blame such men if they were at pains to learn the lingo of the people, and did not trouble their minds with the English language which was used only in the upper classes, few of whom were Catholics and most of whom also spoke or at least understood Patois?' (Devas 1932, 288-289) According to Jean-Baptiste Labat, a French priest in the Dominican Order, he learned the Kéyòl language *'pour comprendre tout ce qu'ils disaient, et pour leur expliquer mes pensées'* ['to understand everything they were saying and to explain my ideas to them'] (Roberts 1997, 138).

Under British rule during the period 1763-1779, the relationship between the British and the French on the island was tense, as the population deeply resented their new British masters. When the French recaptured the island in 1779, the French- and Kéyòl-speaking members of the population were clearly pleased. Father Devas notes that the French in Grenada could not be blamed for being joyful over 'the triumph of their fellow countrymen, or of the people, at least, whose language they spoke and whose religion they shared' (Devas 1974, 74).

By the time the British regained control of Grenada in 1783 for the second and final time, anti-French attitudes on the part of the British had hardened and resentment had grown deeper owing to a number of injustices perpetrated by the French during their second brief period of rule. In addition, the ideas driving the French Revolution of 1789, encapsulated in the words *liberté, égalité, fraternité* (liberty, equality and brotherhood), served to add fuel to the fires of resentment burning brightly on the island of Grenada. The 1800 *Encyclopaedia Britannica* describes Grenada's blacks as being 'tinctured with the love and admiration' of the principles of the French Revolution. Mention is also made of 'the disaffected negroes of Grenada who spoke the French language' (Devas 1974, 117).

These tensions and mutual feelings of hostility between the British and the French set the stage for a very turbulent period in Grenada's history, culminating in 1795 with the Fédon rebellion, an armed insurrection organised by black Grenadians, free people of colour and whites sympathetic to the rebellion's causes. It was led by Julien Fédon, a free coloured Grenadian who owned the Belvidere Estate and laid waste to Grenada from March 1795 to July 1796.

The main factor driving this uprising was the harsh and discriminatory stance adopted by the British towards the French in Grenada in the post-1783 period. The British instituted legal provisions that placed restrictions on the French population's religion (Catholicism), language, voting rights and ability to own land. Anglo-French tensions in Grenada were further heightened by France's declaration of war on Britain on 1 February 1793.

Against this backdrop of repression of the French in Grenada, Julien Fédon began plotting an uprising in 1794. In March of 1795, Fédon and his fighters launched a surprise attack on the settlements of Grenville and Gouyave, killing many British subjects in the process. The British and their supporters sought refuge in St. George's. This attack proved to be merely an opening salvo, as fighting between the French and the British raged on the island for more than one year after that. By January of 1796, Fédon's forces were in control of the entire island, with the exception of St. George's.

In a bid to end the fighting and recapture Grenada from the rebel forces, the British secured massive reinforcements and, in June of 1796, managed to attack and gain control of Fédon's headquarters, named *Camp de la Liberté* (Freedom Camp) and located near his Belvidere Estate. This decisive strike by the British effectively ended the rebellion. Fédon's fighters suffered heavy losses, although Fédon himself, the mastermind behind the rebellion, eluded capture by British forces. To this day, his fate remains a mystery. In the immediate aftermath of the bloody and protracted Fédon rebellion, the British reacted by clamping down on French sympathisers; a number of blacks who were known to have participated in the rebellion were summarily executed, while some free coloureds faced sham trials before suffering the same fate.

In reference to the Fédon rebellion, The *Historical Encyclopaedia of World Slavery* states:

> In all, the revolt involved 150 whites and free coloureds and over 7,000 slaves (roughly half of the island's total).
>
> The rebellion caused an estimated £2.5 million in damage to property and undermined any British hopes that Grenada would become a major sugar producer. In fact, the island largely

reverted to small-scale plantations and peasant agriculture after the uprising. The material devastation, coupled with the psychological shock of the rebellion, caused many whites to leave the island ... the uprising nearly became a Grenadian version of the Haitian revolution. (As cited in Pardue 1997, 266)

Not only did the Fédon rebellion have a lasting impact on Grenada's economic and linguistic fortunes, it also profoundly impacted the psyche of the island's residents.

Returning to the subject of religion, faith and creed were among the most powerful tools used by the British to attack the French. In recounting the 1783-1795 period of Grenada's history, Father Devas notes, in reference to the British, that 'in their eagerness to weaken the French colonists and lessen their power, these men found that the easiest way of achieving this object was by attacking the French in the matter of their religion'. (Devas 1974, 106) In line with this approach, the British began demanding the use of Catholic churches in Grenada and when their demands were resisted, they simply proceeded to seize these churches. There were also attempts to force the Catholic Church to share its revenue with what was called the 'Established Church'.

The Kéyòl-speaking people and the French seem to have forged a strong bond based on anti-British sentiment and religion. Father Devas reports that during this period, a Wesleyan minister attempted to preach to Grenadians, who proceeded to turn their backs on this preacher and, referring to Catholicism, stated 'we like our religion best'.

In the widespread and forceful attempt by the British to wipe out everything French in Grenada, language failed to be spared. The all-out effort waged by the British to rid Grenada of its French legacy was a phenomenon unseen in other Caribbean islands that became British possessions after years of French rule. Peter Roberts sums up the impact of colonial rivalry in Grenada thus:

The most important factor in language change in Grenada was the bitter antagonism that developed in Grenada itself between the French and the English in the years between 1763 and 1795. Up until 1763 the French alone had controlled Grenada. From

1763 to 1779 it was a British possession. In 1779 the French recaptured the island and held it until 1783. The British regained it in 1783 and held it until 1795, a year which saw the culmination of the antagonism when an attempt was made in the name of the French Republic to recapture the island. (Roberts 1997, 90-91)

Roberts goes on to observe that 'the antagonism between the two colonial powers in Grenada was not normal or characteristic' (Roberts 1997, 91).

In one of my interviews with an elderly Grenadian Kéyòl speaker, she recounted a childhood practice of feuding children insulting each other with the Kéyòl words *anglé kochon* [French: *cochon anglais*; English: English pig] and *fwansé kabwit* [French: *cabri français*; English: French goat]. These terms seem to corroborate the view that the deep hostility between the French and British in Grenada did in fact colour the views of Kéyòl speakers.

Fierce colonial rivalry and fighting between the British and the French and the intense animus between these two powers no doubt played a significant role in the decline of Kéyòl in Grenada. As mentioned above, the erosion of the Kéyòl language was not an overnight affair; the disappearance of a language is always gradual. In fact, Kéyòl continued to be the *lingua franca* of the island throughout the nineteenth century and into the early part of the twentieth century. The influence of French priests on the island and the interaction with other islands, including Trinidad, where French-lexicon Creole was also the dominant language of communication during that period, would also have worked in favour of the preservation of the language during this period.

In the final analysis, however, when the British emerged as the victors in the bitter quest for control of Grenada, the hostility of the British in Grenada towards the French and, by extension, the Kéyòl language, owing to rebellion and religion, ultimately hastened the decline of the Kéyòl language.

Migration

As discussed earlier, Trinidad's second and more successful *Cédula de Población* was issued on 24 November 1783. This year coincided with the capture of Grenada by the British. Frenchmen who found life in Grenada unbearable and oppressive under British rule migrated to Trinidad, taking their enslaved workers with them. When the bloody Fédon rebellion ended in 1796 and the British prevailed, the pace of migration of Grenadians of French origin and their Kéyòl-speaking workforce appears to have picked up, as the former group fled the island, fearing British reprisals and retaliation. Though the numbers are not known, a significant percentage of the French- and Kéyòl-speaking Grenadian population is thought to have left the island, taking their languages with them.

In addition, Grenada has historically had a stubbornly high rate of migration, as Grenadians have a tradition of leaving their island in large numbers in search of better opportunities. Nearby Trinidad has always been a lure for Grenadians, even in modern times. A number of other destinations have been popular during different periods. In the 1940s and 1950s, many Grenadians went to Curaçao and Aruba, in the 1950s and 1960s to England, and from the 1970s to the present to North America, and particularly the United States. If my own experience can be used as a guide, of my roughly 60 classmates who completed secondary school with me, roughly 10 are currently living in Grenada. It is significant that Haiti's King Henri Christophe (1767-1820), who made his mark on that country's history, was Grenadian, as was Louise Little, the mother of Malcolm X. If a language is to remain stable, its people must be stable. Grenadians' high rate of migration therefore had a detrimental effect on the Kéyòl language, as people departed for distant shores. This point clearly hit home during my discussions on the French-lexicon Creole language with Nnamdi Hodge. The French-lexicon-Creole-speaking diaspora includes the Güiria and Macuro communities in Venezuela, where Mr Hodge interviewed a number of French-lexicon Creole speakers. Amazingly, one of the speakers of this language has the last name Briceño, and this gentleman traces his origins back to the Brizan family in Grenada, where he lived for a number of years. (See video **Chapter 6: Social Dimensions of Kéyòl**; *Migration and the Decline of Grenada's Kéyòl* video clip.)

Grenada: A Hub of Activity

In the 1700s, Grenada was strategically important in that it served as a stopover point for ships trading between the different islands and the South American mainland. Trade always has a great impact on language and it is reasonable to believe that, from the standpoint of trade, the British presence in Grenada in the latter part of the century would have had the effect of eroding the Kéyòl language.

Another factor that would have accelerated the decline of Kéyòl is the fact that Grenada served as the administrative headquarters of the British Windward Islands from 1885 to 1958. This would have led the English language to assume even greater importance in Grenada's linguistic landscape, as most administrative business would have been conducted in English, once again to the detriment of the Kéyòl language.

The above factors, taken together, explain why the number of fluent Kéyòl speakers in Grenada has fallen precipitously over the past 80 years or so, to the point where the sun is rapidly setting on this beautiful language. (See video **Chapter 7: Conversation between Two Kéyòl Speakers in Grenada**; *Conversation between Two Kéyòl Speakers in Grenada* video clip.)

3

MODERN-DAY KÉYÒL INFLUENCES IN GRENADA

Despite the fact that the Kéyòl language is on the verge of disappearance in Grenada, its linguistic influence remains very much present in modern-day Grenadian English-lexicon Creole. This influence is clearly discernible in the voice inflections of Grenadians when they speak English, in their pronunciation of certain words and in the many Kéyòl-derived loan words used in everyday speech. Furthermore, Grenadians' ways of expressing themselves in Grenadian English-lexicon Creole often follow Kéyòl speech patterns and grammatical structures. In 1990, M.G. Smith, in a co-authored publication entitled 'Education and Society in the Creole Caribbean', made the observation that in Grenada 'though the older generation that used the French patois had passed away, their descendants communicated among themselves in a form of English strongly influenced by the French-based Creole'.

Some of the Kéyòl influences on Grenadian English-lexicon Creole are demonstrated below.

Grenadian English-lexicon Creole

Relexification in everyday speech. Relexification is defined as a process where one language replaces most or all of its lexicon (words) with the words of another language, without significantly changing the grammar. This is clearly seen in the shift from Grenadian Kéyòl to Grenadian English-lexicon Creole over the years. English words have replaced French-derived words, while grammatical structures have often remained fairly intact.

Some examples of relexification in Grenadian English-lexicon Creole are provided below.

Grenadian English-lexicon Creole	Kéyòl
She makin baby	*I ka fè popo*
It make hot today	*I ka fè cho jodi-a*
How they callin you? [What is your name?]	*Kouman yé ka kiyé ou?*
It had two boys in the yard	*I té tini dé gason an lakou-a*
He have ten years	*I tini dis lané*
I does go in the market on Saturdays	*Mwen ka alé market toulé samdi*
Miss me! [said by someone who does not want to get drawn into a controversy]	*Chapé mwen*
You too frontish ['frontish' in Grenadian English-lexicon Creole means 'meddlesome' or 'pushy']	*Ou douvan twòp*
For true?	*Pou vwé?*
Beat you mouth [to talk incessantly]	*Bat bouch*
Band you belly [to gird oneself for difficulty]	*Mawé bouden*
Put water in a person's eyes [to bring tears to someone's eyes]	*Mété dlo nan zyé* (Winer 2009, 734)
After one time is another	*Apwé yon tan sé lòt*

God is in charge	*Papa bondjé, sé mèt*
Make a jail	*Fè ladjòl*
Which part ['Which part' is synonymous with the interrogative 'where']	*Ki koté*
Foreday mornin	*Douvan jou*
To take in front before in front take you	*Pwan douvan avan douvan pwan ou*
I there [I'm okay]	*Mwen la*
Outside woman [mistress]	*Fam déwò*
A mister	*Yon misyé*
What do you? [What is wrong with you?]	*Sa ki fè ou?*
Big people [adults]	*Gran moun*
How much for that?	*Kouman pou sa?*
Bring it give me [Bring it to me]	*Méné li ba mwen*
Cut you backside [to spank]	*Koupé dèyè-ou*

Use of tags or markers. In Grenadian English-lexicon Creole, the tags *wi* [French: *oui;* English: yes], *non* [French: *non*; English: no] and *ki* [French: *qui*; English: which] are often heard in daily speech. It should be noted that the tags *wi* and *non* are used in Grenadian English-lexicon Creole to stress or emphasise an idea. The tag *ki* is generally used in Grenadian English-lexicon Creole in a mocking way, to express scepticism.

The following are examples of the use of tags or markers in Grenadian English-lexicon Creole:

1. I goin down the road, **wi**.
2. Behave yourself **non,** boy!
3. She say she gettin married next year. **Ki** married? Somebody go marry that girl?

Storytelling and Folklore

In form and content, Caribbean storytelling has often been traced to Africa. Wherever African people or people of African ancestry are found, storytelling features prominently. Though not nearly as common as it once was, storytelling is still alive in the rural parts of Grenada. Grenadian folklore and stories are replete with Kéyòl words that are sometimes taken from characters found in African tales or stories. In Grenada, Nansi (Anansi) stories are still alive. Anansi, a trickster in West African tales, generally takes the form of a spider who lives by his wits and consistently outsmarts his opponents. Grenadian Nansi stories generally have two main characters: Kompè Zayen [French: *araignée*; English: spider] and Kompè Tig [French: *tigre*; English: tiger]. Kompè Zayen is equivalent to Anansi, the swindler. Nansi stories are usually told in a call-and-response format, with the narrator opening the story with the words *cric (krik)* and the audience responding *crac (krak)* or *tim tim* and the audience responding with *bwa sèk* [French: *bois sec*; English: dry wood].

Grenadian folklore and mythology revolve around frightfully vivid stories of characters, many of which have Kéyòl names.

The *ligarou* [French: *loup garou*; English: werewolf] in Grenadian folklore is believed to have the ability to transform itself from a human being into all manner of ferocious animals and the power to cast evil spells on people.

A *ladjablès* [French: *la diablesse*; English: she-devil] is a tall, beautiful woman with erect posture who trolls lonely, dark roads, her face concealed under a wide-brimmed hat in search of victims. She wears a long skirt to conceal her feet, one of which is a cloven hoof. She is believed to lure men deep into forests, from which they sometimes never emerge.

There is also the *soukouyan*, a word derived from the West African Soninke language (*sukunya* refers to a sorcerer). (Winer 2009, 838) In Grenadian folklore, a *soukouyan* is believed to be an old woman who sleeps by day and sheds her wrinkled skin in the evening, transforming herself into a ball of fire as darkness descends and she goes off to suck the blood of her victims. She must return to the skin she has shed before day breaks. The sprinkling of salt where she may tread is believed to keep her at bay. The notion of humans shedding their skin is thought to be derived from the Yoruba religion.

Mama maladi [French: *maman maladie*; English: mother of sickness] is believed to be the spirit of a woman who died in childbirth. She wanders aimlessly at night making the sound of a crying baby. It is believed that anyone who tries to get a glimpse of her will be spirited away, never to be seen again.

Mama glo [French: *maman de l'eau*; English: mother of the water]. The concept is derived from one of the gods (*orishas*) of the Yoruba religion, Yemanja, the spirit of the water, and is associated with the Yoruba-derived Shango religion in Grenada. Outside of the Shango community, the term *mama glo* has become secularised, with most Grenadians viewing the term *mama glo* as a reference to a mermaid. (See video **Chapter 5: Storytelling and Folklore**; *Discussion* video clip.)

Proverbs and Idioms

Proverbs occupy an important place in the culture of Africa, given this continent's strong oral traditions. One of the clearest links between Africa and the Caribbean is the love of proverbs and idioms, the tendency to speak in symbolic terms and to couch observations and insights in concise, figurative language in order to impart universal truths and wisdom. Grenadian Calypsonian The Mighty Sparrow, whose contribution to Kéyòl and calypso is discussed below, captures the Caribbean predilection for proverbs in his calypso 'Parables'. The song opens with the following words: 'Long ago, when I was young/and anything at all go wrong/I used to run to me grandmother/she used to help me, but brother/when she talk is only parable....' In his book *From Oral to Literate Culture: Colonial Experience in the English West Indies*, Peter Roberts notes that the slaves' facility with language and their ability to encapsulate general truths in short sentences seemed to surprise Europeans (Roberts 1997, 44). In fact, John Stewart, an English writer, observes that the sayings of the enslaved 'often convey an astonishing force and meaning' (Roberts 1997, 44).

Regardless of the Caribbean island and the European linguistic influence, there is a striking similarity between proverbs and idioms from one island to the next which, in my view, can be explained only by a shared African ancestry. In some cases, the words and the message are virtually the same; in others, different words are used to convey the same message. Referring to the fact that not every smile or laugh is genuine, the Jamaican English-lexicon Creole proverb is 'A nuh every kin teet a laugh'. In Grenadian English-lexicon Creole, the proverb is quite similar, both in words and meaning: 'All skin teeth is not grin'. Another example is the Jamaican English-lexicon Creole proverb 'Duppy know who fi frighten'. Here, the Grenadian and Trinidadian English-lexicon Creole equivalent is 'Monkey know what tree to climb'. In this instance, the words are different, but the message is exactly the same: a bully tends to attack those perceived as weak or unlikely to strike back. Another example is Guadeloupe, Grenada and Jamaica (among others), which share the common idiom *djèl-kabwit* (French-lexicon Creole) or 'goat-mouth' (English-lexicon Creole), referring to someone who speaks about or wishes for a negative outcome that actually comes to pass. It seems quite likely that these sayings were introduced by Africans on the individual Caribbean islands to which they were transported rather than being transferred from island to island.

Trinidadian John Jacob Thomas, whose invaluable contribution to our knowledge of French-lexicon Creole is discussed later on, described this language's proverbs as 'the beautiful sayings which form the ornament of African discourse' (Thomas 1969, 120). In the specific case of Grenada, many of the island's proverbs and idioms were originally expressed in Kéyòl and entered Grenadian English-lexicon Creole over the years, often in relexified form.

Below are examples of Grenadian Kéyòl proverbs and idioms that are now expressed in Grenadian English-lexicon Creole. Many of these are common to other Caribbean islands. Where considered necessary, explanations are provided in brackets.

1. *Ti kochon té mandé mama poutji djèl long kon sa, mama wéponn li 'vini ou ka vini, ou ka wè'*
   Little pig ask it mother why it mouth so long, and it mother say 'is come you comin, you go see'
   [Experience and age teach wisdom]

2. *Wazyè tini zòwèy*
   Bush have ears

3. *Ki mélé zé nan kalinda-wòch*
   Egg have no right in rock stone dance
   [When there is contact between the strong and the weak, the weak will be crushed]

4. *Sak vide pa ka tjenn doubout*
   Empty [crocus] bag can't stand up
   [Substance is important]

5. *Mama ka fè ich, mé pa tjè-yé*
   Mother does make children but not their hearts

6. *Makak sav ki pyé-bwa i ka monté*
   Monkey know what tree to climb
   [Bullies attack the weak]

7. *Bat tambou épi dansé li* (Thomas 1969, 117)
   To beat one's drum and dance to its beat

8. *Pwan dité pou lafyèv-yon moun* (Thomas 1969, 119)
   To drink bush for someone's fever
   [To take up someone else's cause or fight as one's own]

9. *Tout moun mété lamen nan bouch* (Thomas 1969, 120)
   Everybody put hand to mouth
   [A physical gesture expressing shock or disbelief]

10. *Tan moun konnèt nan gran jou, nannwit pa bizwen chandèl pou kléwé yo* (Thomas 1969, 125)
    What you know in the day, you don't need candle to see in the night

11. *Sa ki sla-ou, sé sla-ou*
    What is yours is yours

12. *Chyen pa ka fè chat*
    Dog don't make cat
    [The fruit does not fall far from the tree]

13. *Sa zyé pa wè, tjè pa ka fè mal*
    What the eyes don't see don't hurt the heart

14. *Sé kòd-yam ki mawé yam*
    Is the yam vine that does tie up the yam
    [Problems emanate from within one's own circle]

15. *Wè pou kò-ou* (Allsopp 2003, 596)
    Beware! Watch out!

16. *Apwé wi, sé pléwé*
    After joy, is sorrow

17. *Bèl dan pa di zami*
    All skin teeth is not grin

18. *Dé mal kwab pa ka viv an mem twou*
    Two man crab can't live in the same hole

19. *La bèf mawé, sé la i ka manjé*
    Where you tie cow is where it go eat

20. *Mayé tini dan*
    Marriage have teeth

21. *Padon pa djéri bòs*
    Sorry can't cure it

22. *Lamè pa tini bwanch*
    Sea water don't have branch

23. *Djab pa ka domi*
    The devil doesn't sleep

Folk Songs, Carnival and Calypso

To some degree, Grenada's Kéyòl is being preserved in song, particularly in folk songs. The Grenadian group Palé Patwa LaGwinad has done a commendable job of preserving and expanding Grenada's Kéyòl songs through cultural performances on the island. Nnamdi Hodge, a Trinidadian who spent a number of his formative years in Grenada, has carried out and continues to carry out extensive research on Lesser Antillean French-lexicon Creole in general and on Trinidad's French-lexicon Creole in particular. In 2009, Hodge and Florence Blizzard co-compiled a songbook titled *Vini Chanté an Patwa* (*Come Sing in Patois*), a wonderful collection of French-lexicon Creole songs sung in Trinidad, accompanied by a CD. Some of the songs on this CD were once common in Grenada and are still sung or at least recognised by the elderly. They include *Dodo Piti Popo* and *I Ka Boucan*. (See video **Chapter 3: Folk Songs**; *Dodo Piti Popo* video clip.)

The folk song below, known as Exilia, was once very common in Grenada. The chorus may still be familiar to some:

Exilia chorus

Oy-yo yo yo yo, Exilia

Ay-yay, yay, yay, yay, Exilia

Si ou émé mwen pou mayé

Mandé sésé mwen

(See video **Chapter 3: Folk Songs**; *Exilia* video clip.)

Another is *Chat Ki Manjé Lamowi-a*, a song that was sometimes sung to accompany *kwadril* [French: *quadrille*] dancing. The *kwadril* dance dates back to early eighteenth-century France. The French-style *kwadril* dance in Grenada and Carriacou is thought to have remained fairly intact; it has not undergone significant adaptation. This dance remains very popular in Carriacou. (See video **Chapter 3: Folk Songs**; *Chat Ki Manjé Lamowi-a* video clip.)

Yet another, less common, folk song is *Jou Ka Ouvè*, which sings about the dawn of a new day. (See video **Chapter 3: Folk Songs**; *Jou Ka Ouvè* video clip.)

Folk songs are therefore an important dimension of Grenada's culture. Historically, they are also important, as they once served as an accompaniment to and a soothing balm for the tedious, back-breaking work of the enslaved and, later, as a form of community entertainment. The influence which the Kéyòl language has exerted upon them is clear.

Carnival also bears the imprint of the Kéyòl language and is thought to have been introduced to Grenada by French Catholic plantation owners during the 1700s. For the French, carnival was a lavish indoor masked ball. The African workforce was, of course, excluded from these festivities; for them, carnival quickly became an outdoor festival that offered a brief respite from their harsh daily working conditions.

More importantly, carnival provided the enslaved with an outlet for their pent-up frustrations as well as an opportunity to celebrate and express their own African culture. Given the repression associated with slavery, these frustrations were conveyed in indirect ways—often by poking fun at or engaging in veiled mockery and ridicule of their masters.

In the early days, Grenada's carnival involved drumming, percussion instruments, singing and stick fighting (*kalinda*). *Kalinda* stick fighting has exerted a significant influence over the modern-day carnival. *Kalinda* performances were often accompanied by the *tambou bambou* (bamboo drum). Drums have always been important to people of African ancestry. In Grenada and other Caribbean islands, African workers once used drums to communicate with each other, to express themselves culturally and to entertain their communities. Drumming remains an integral part of the island's modern-day culture, where the Tivoli Drummers often occupy centre stage at cultural shows. The *tambou bambou* drums also helped lay the groundwork for the emergence of the modern steel pan instrument.

With the emancipation of the enslaved in the Anglophone islands in 1834, carnival assumed greater importance. Although this festival was initially associated with the lower classes, it gained greater acceptance over time as its artistic, cultural and historical value came to be recognised and appreciated. Today, carnival is embraced by all levels of society. In fact, in Grenada and in other islands, particularly in Trinidad, apart from being a major tourist draw, this festival has morphed into a vibrant form of street theatre, a cultural and artistic extravaganza and a fleeting opportunity to escape life's sorrows and enjoy a period of spontaneous revelry.

Grenada has retained many Kéyòl words that are associated with carnival. One of these is *kanboulé* [French: *cannes brûlées*; English: burnt cane], a word thought to be associated with the burning of cane fields, either accidentally or intentionally, during the period of slavery. It later came to be associated with the celebrations marking emancipation from slavery, with these celebrations being incorporated into carnival. (It should be noted that the French origin of the word *kanboulé* is not universally accepted; the term is believed by some to be derived from the Congo word *kambule*, meaning 'procession'.)

Additional Kéyòl words associated with carnival in Grenada are:

Jouvé [French: *jour ouvert*; English: day break]

Djab [French: *diable*; English: devil]

Dimanch gwa [French: *dimanche gras*; English: Fat (or Shrove) Sunday]

Vyéko [French: *vieux corps*; English: old body]

Djamèt [French: *diamètre*; English: diameter], referring to the divisions of society, with a *djamèt* coming from the lower societal levels.

Lawa fré fré [French: *le roi*; English: the king, and probably French: *se frayer*; English: to fight one's way through a situation], referring to the *kalinda* stick fighters who duelled with each other for the title of king.

Given the historically close connection between carnival and the Kéyòl language, a description of the traditional carnival or masquerade genres is provided below. Some genres have proved more enduring than others.

Kalinda, a blend of martial arts and dancing, has its roots in Africa. In a flamboyant display of agility and dexterity, two men duel with sticks until a winner emerges. Though *kalinda* now takes place only at carnival time, *kalinda* stick fighters once performed on any special occasion in Grenada. For example, when a new rum shop was opened, particularly in the rural areas, *kalinda* stick fighters were invited to perform outside the shop to promote and draw attention to the new business. The songs sung during *kalinda* performances were often in Kéyòl. *Kalinda*, which emerged in a context of slavery, bears some similarity to the Brazilian *capoeira* dance that incorporates martial arts. (See video **Chapter 4: Carnival and Calypso**; *Kalinda (Song)* video clip.)

The *bwa-bwa* [French: *bois*; English: wood] is very similar to the modern-day *moko jumbie* masquerader. The main difference between the two is that with the *bwa-bwa*, the stilts used to support the dancers extended right up to the latter's arms; they held on to the sticks with their hands to obtain extra support. The *moko jumbie* has no support; he walks only on stilts.

The *djab djab* is one of the most enduring genres of masquerader, although a number of features have changed over the years. The main aim of the *djab djab* is to be as devil-like as possible in order to instil fear in onlookers. Originally, *djab djabs* covered their bodies with ground charcoal mixed with lard and put red colouring in their mouths to make their appearance as frightening as possible. They would sometimes carry large snakes around their necks, and would convert a chamber pot (called a *po* in Grenadian Kéyòl [French: *pot de chambre*; English: chamber pot]) into a hat by inverting it on their heads and attaching horns to it. Dragging chains and mock coffins along, they once performed in communities by pretending to read from books and spelling often lewd words out loud. Once they were finished entertaining the crowd, they would then pass around a pouch on a long wooden stick to collect money. The *djab djabs* would pretend to chase and scare the more parsimonious onlookers who were reluctant to make a donation. Originally, many of the *djab djab* chants were in Kéyòl. (See video **Chapter 4: Carnival and Calypso**; *Djab Djab (Chant)* video clip.) Modern-day *djab djabs* are basically revellers who apply some form of black (or blue, yellow or green) paint to their bodies and dance in the streets at carnival time, having dispensed with most of the *djab djab* paraphernalia over the years. While the blowing of the *lambi* (conch) shell is associated with *jouvé* morning in general, it is more frequently blown by the *djab djabs*.

Illustration 3.1 A *djab djab* huddle on *jouvé* morning
Jouvé festivities take place on Carnival Monday.

The *short-knee* masqueraders come from the Victoria (parish of St. Mark) and Chantimelle (parish of St. Patrick) areas of Grenada. These masqueraders wear a small mesh mask and colourful, loose clothing adorned with small mirrors. They sprinkle powder on themselves and onlookers as they sing and dance through the streets. They play no musical instruments; instead they dance to the rhythm of their ankle bells. Their songs are sung in a call-and-response format, with a *chantwèl* [French: *chanterelle*; English: E-string (of the violin)] playing the role of lead singer.

The *Paywo* [French: *Pierrot*] masqueraders' name is derived from Italian *Commedia dell'arte* performances, which were popular in late seventeenth-century France. These outdoor, slapstick-style performances were often improvised, and one of the characters, the *Pierrot*, was a buffoonish jester who whitened his face with powder and wore loose, baggy outfits. In Grenada, the *Paywo*, who has disappeared from modern-day carnival, used to portray himself as a comedic scholar. He entertained carnival onlookers by reciting long passages or providing sly commentary on village affairs. The modern-day short-knee masquerader is linked to the earlier *Paywo*. The masks and some aspects of the *Paywo* and short-knee costumes are quite similar. In Carriacou, the popular *Shakespeare mas* (the term generally used in Grenada and a number of other Caribbean islands to refer to masquerade) is derived from the *Paywo*. The Trinidadian *Paywo Gwinad* [French: *Pierrot Grenade;* English*:* Grenada *Pierrot*] has the same origin.

Carriacou's Shakespeare masquerader gives the island's carnival a distinctive flavour. On Carnival Tuesday [French: *mardi gras*; English: Shrove Tuesday], these masqueraders parade in the streets of Carriacou reciting passages from Shakespeare (*Julius Caesar* is the most popular) and other historical works. They travel in pairs and the slightest oratorical slip on the part of the narrator earns him a flogging (generally given in a theatrical and jesting manner) with the whip carried by his companion. Shakespeare masqueraders wear crowns on their heads that have extensions made of pieces of thick, starched, waist-length fabric to protect their upper bodies from the blows they receive. When a Shakespeare masquerader completes his narration, onlookers generally applaud and blow *lambi* shells to express their appreciation and approval. The whips and costumes of the Carriacou *Paywo* are very reminiscent of the Trinidadian *Paywo Gwinad.*

The history masquerader once paraded through the streets of Grenada reciting passages from Shakespeare and episodes of British history dressed in costumes reminiscent of Shakespearen Great Britain. Grenada's now defunct history masquerader and Carriacou's current Shakespeare masquerader are virtually one and the same.

The maypole dancers come largely from the parishes of St. David and St. Andrew in Grenada. Dressed in colourful clothing, they erect a pole and sing and dance in skilful formations that lead to the plaiting and unplaiting of the pole. Some maypole songs are still sung in Kéyòl.

The vyékos come from Victoria (parish of St. Mark) and Gouyave (parish of St. John). The *vyékos* from Victoria wear wooden clogs and dark, loose, ragged clothing, often made of burlap. They sometimes wear an inverted chamber pot with a single horn on their heads. They drag old pans and tins along as they parade through the streets. They have no musical instruments; they dance to the rhythmic sound made by their clogs. The dark clothing of the Victoria *vyékos*, which is sometimes adorned with crosses, and their precise, rhythmic stomping create a funereal aura during carnival parades. Some aspects of their dress are reminiscent of that of the *djab djabs*. The costumes of the Gouyave *vyékos* tend be more colourful. These *vyékos* focus more on the darker side of human nature, with their carnival bands having names like 'Devils from Hell' and 'Devil's Angels'. They sometimes wear hoods over their heads and drag coffins along in their parades. The Gouyave *vyékos* consistently present good as triumphing over evil.

Illustration 3.2
A hooded *vyéko* dances to the stomping sound of his clogs
The *vyéko* is a traditional carnival masquerader in Grenada.

The wild Indians wear colourful costumes—skirts, crowns or feathered headdresses, nose beads and long rope braids. The brightly coloured paint applied to their bodies once came from the dye extracted from the seeds of the *roukou* plant, a practice inherited from Grenada's indigenous people. They generally play no musical instruments; they sing songs and, in the past, pretended to be untamed and uncontrollable, running into the bushes to hide when money was thrown at them by crowds before they regrouped again to continue dancing. Someone in the group would subsequently collect the money. (See video **Chapter 4: Carnival and Calypso**; *Wild Indian* (*Song*) video clip.)

Calypso is another fertile ground for Kéyòl. Traditional calypsos are essentially social and political commentary in song. It is for this reason that calypso was once known as the newspaper of the poor. Calypso and Kéyòl are closely linked, as all calypsos were originally sung in this language. The use of calypso as a vehicle for social commentary has largely continued, with Calypsonians often singing about topical events using lyrics laced with humour, satire, irreverence and, quite often, a healthy dose of raunchiness.

As late as the 1960s, when Kéyòl had ceased to be the *lingua franca* in Grenada, some calypsos were still being sung in Kéyòl. While this language was initially used because it was the medium of communication with which Calypsonians in the late 1800s and early 1900s were most comfortable, by the 1950s and 1960s, when Kéyòl's heyday was over, there may have been other reasons for singing calypsos in Kéyòl. In the context of slavery, frustration and anger could not be overtly expressed. Against such a backdrop, coded communication became commonplace. For historical and social reasons, therefore, Calypsonians have always resorted to clever word play and *double entendre* to comment on social or political events or to discuss sexual or amorous matters that would be frowned upon or considered coarse or lewd if tackled openly. It therefore seems likely that the Calypsonians who opted to compose calypsos in the Kéyòl language in the 1950s and 1960s were using this language as a cover to transmit veiled political messages or to brag about sexual exploits or encounters, both real and imagined. It should be borne in mind that during the 1950s and 1960s, many adults in Grenada were still able to understand and even speak Kéyòl, even though children generally could not. Peter Roberts, in his book *From Oral to Literate Culture: Colonial Experience in the English West Indies*, correctly observes:

> In the case of the Calypsonian, in addition to the pride of being able to manipulate words, there is the necessity to talk about the details of sex without being branded indecent or to talk about politicians without being victimised … This practice of double

meaning or nondirect communication arises out of a social situation in which class conflict (today) and the master/slave relationship (previously) have prevented the powerless from speaking frankly or directly to the powerful. (Roberts 1997, 8)

This comment rings particularly true in a country like Grenada where, even today, people tend not to speak to each other in frank terms or to express their frustrations in a direct and open manner because of not only the legacy of slavery and class conflict but also the island's small size and thus the close connections between Grenadians. In everyday life in Grenada, displeasure or disapproval is often expressed by 'throwing words' (making comments intended for an individual without directly addressing him or her) or by using idioms or proverbs.

Any discussion of calypso would be incomplete without paying tribute to Slinger Francisco, D.Litt., the Calypsonian better known as The Mighty Sparrow or Birdie, considered by many to be the King of Calypso. A Grenadian by birth, Sparrow started composing calypsos in the 1950s. His genius as a songwriter continues to this day. A master of wit, word play, repartee, raunchiness and *double entendre*, Sparrow, who has spent most of his adult life in Trinidad, deserves a special place of honour in the annals of Caribbean history and culture, given the immeasurable contribution he has made to promoting the visibility of the art form of calypso through his rich and varied repertoire of several hundred songs. Indeed, Sparrow's versatility and use of song to comment on a wide range of global political and social issues speak eloquently to his artistic genius. He will go down in history as one of the Caribbean's greatest musical giants and as someone who made a singular contribution to the development of calypso by breaking down barriers and throwing open doors, thus putting calypso on the global map.

The lyrics of a number of Sparrow's early calypsos were wholly or partly in Kéyòl. Calypso lovers will certainly harbour fond memories of Sparrow's *Sa Sa Yé*, *Gadé Zahina*, *Lévé Mako*, *Manjé* and *Kiyé Mwen*.

Sparrow's *Gadé Zahina* deals with the sometimes fraught relationships between men and women, a common theme in calypsos, both past and present. The lyrics of this song, which appear below with their Grenadian English-lexicon Creole translations, may be familiar to some.

GADÉ ZAHINA

By

THE MIGHTY SPARROW (1970)

KÉYÒL	GRENADIAN ENGLISH-LEXICON CREOLE
Verse 1 On tifi vlé pou mayé mwen I ka fè yon ich, di mwen sé papa-i Jenn tifi sa ki fè ou fou? Mwen pa konné ayen kon sa	Verse 1 A girl want to marry me She makin baby and sayin I is the father Young girl, you crazy? I don't know anything about that
Chorus Gadé Zahina, woy, woy Gadé Zahina, woy, woy Gadé Zahina, woy, woy Gadé Zahina, woy, woy Gadé Zahina fè yon konplo Pou tjwé mwen, woy, woy	Chorus Look at Zahina, woy, woy Look at Zahina, woy, woy Look at Zahina, woy, woy Look at Zahina, woy, woy Look Zahina come up with a plot To kill me, woy, woy
Verse 2 Sése-li épi mama-li épi Nonk-li di mwen pa alé Fouté mwen yon mòso bwa I ka tjwé mwen si mwen pa mayé	Verse 2 Her sister, mother and Uncle tell me not to leave They hit me with a piece of wood She go kill me if I don't marry her
(Chorus)	(Chorus)
Verse 3 Kasé tèt-mwen, é kasé pyé-mwen E mwen vlé kouwi, twòp chyen déwò Bondjé fè i tombé asou bouden-an Sé li ki mò	Verse 3 She buss me head and break me foot I wanted to run, but dog for so outside God make her fall on her belly And is she that dead
(Chorus)	(Chorus)

Religion and Spirituality

The French presence in Grenada for over a century has resulted in a strong Roman Catholic contingent on the island; roughly 60 percent of the population is Catholic. The other dominant religion is Anglicanism (Church of England), introduced by the British after England wrested control of Grenada from France. The island also has a smaller number of followers of the Methodist, Presbyterian, Seventh Day Adventist and Pentecostal denominations. In recent years, however, Catholicism has been losing ground to other religious denominations. The presence and influence of French priests in Grenada have already been discussed. Kéyòl and, in some cases, the French language were once the medium of spiritual expression and worship in Grenada. Older Grenadians in general and Catholics in particular still remember prayers and hymns in French, as well as Kéyòl songs sung at wakes, which were known as *lakampayn*. These wakes were essentially community gatherings organised to pray for and honour the life of the deceased and are now known in Grenada as 'three nights' prayers' and 'nine nights' prayers' as they are held three and nine nights after the death of an individual. (See video **Chapter 2: Religious and Spiritual Expression**; *Lakampayn (Prayer for the Deceased)*: *Discussion and Songs* and *Catholicism* video clips.)

Perhaps it is in the spiritual sphere that Africa's influence on Grenadians is most evident, intact and enduring. Shango, one of the deities of the Yoruba religion, has survived in Grenada from the era of slavery and the immediate post-emancipation period, when West Africans were brought to Grenada under the indentured labour system (in the 1850s), to the present times. Currently, it is practised mainly in the rural areas of the island. Shango is one of many *orishas* (manifestations of God in the Yoruba spiritual or religious system) and represents the god of fire, lightning and thunder. Owing to the influence of colonial attitudes and thinking, Shango, the religion that provides the most direct link between the people of Grenada and Africa, is still looked down upon in Grenada. In fact, as late as 1990, there were laws on the books of Grenada prohibiting the practice of Shango and 'shouting' baptism. However, despite the scorn and ridicule heaped on this religion, it has managed to hold its own among a segment of the Grenadian population and to be passed on from generation to generation for over 150 years. The truth is that it is a rich and important part of the history and heritage of Grenadians and thus deserves greater respect and visibility. The Kéyòl language is used in some of the songs sung at Shango ceremonies, as demonstrated in this book's companion video. (See video **Chapter 2: Religious and Spiritual Expression**; *Shango: Discussion and Songs* video clip.)

While the influence of Kéyòl on Christmas festivities in Grenada seems to have waned significantly, the elderly Kéyòl speakers interviewed in Grenada were able to recall a few Christmas songs, which have been included in the video accompanying this book. (See video **Chapter 2: Religious and Spiritual Expression**; *Christmas Serenading (songs)* video clip.)

Toponyms

The abundance of French toponyms in Grenada reflects the enduring French influence on the island. Most Grenadians would be familiar with such place names as Beaulieu, Perdmontemps, Point Salines, Grand Étang and Sans Souci; however, many would be surprised at the sheer length of the list of French or French-derived toponyms in Grenada and Carriacou. A fairly comprehensive list is provided below. The spellings appearing here reflect those widely used or accepted in Grenada. Diacritical marks have been added to certain words as a pronunciation guide.

French-derived Toponyms in Grenada, Carriacou and Petite Martinique

ANSE LA ROCHE BAY (CARRIACOU)	APRÈS TOUT
BAY À L'EAU (CARRIACOU)	BEAULIEU
BEAUREGARD	BEAUSÉJOUR

BELAIR (CARRIACOU)	BELLE ISLE
BELLE PLAINE	BELLEVUE
BELMONT	BELVIDÈRE
BONAIR	BOULOGNE
CAFÉ	CALLISTE
CARRIÈRE	CASTAIGNE
CÉLESTE	CHADEAU
CHAMPS FLEURS	CHANTIMELLE
CHAPEAU CARRÉ (CARRIACOU)	CLOZIER
CONCORD	CORBEAU [TOWN]
CROCHU	DARBEAU
DEPONTHIEU [STREET]	DUQUESNE

Illustration 3.3 Signage for Duquesne Bay
Kalinago petroglyphs can be found in Duquesne Bay.

FALAISE	FONTENOY
GOUYAVE	GRAND ANSE
GRAND BRAS	GRAND ÉTANG
GRAND MAL	GRAND ROY
GROS POINT	JEAN ANGLAIS
L'ESPÉRANCE	L'ESTERRE (CARRIACOU)
LA BAYE	LA CHAUSSÉE

LA DIGUE	LA FEMME
LA FILLETTE	LA FORTUNE
LA MODE	LA POTERIE
LA SAGESSE	LA TANTE
LA TASTE	LABORIE
LANCE AUX EPINES	MAMMA CANNES
MARDIGRAS	MARIGOT
MARQUIS	MIRABEAU
MOLINIÈRE	MON PLAISIR
MON REPOS	MONT TOUT
MONTREUIL	MORNE DÉLICE
MORNE FENDUE	MORNE GOZO
MORNE JALOUX	MORNE LONGUE
MORNE ROCHE	MORNE ROUGE
MORNE TRANQUILLE	MOUNT CENIS

NIANGANFOIX	NONPAREIL
PALMISTE	PERDMONTEMPS

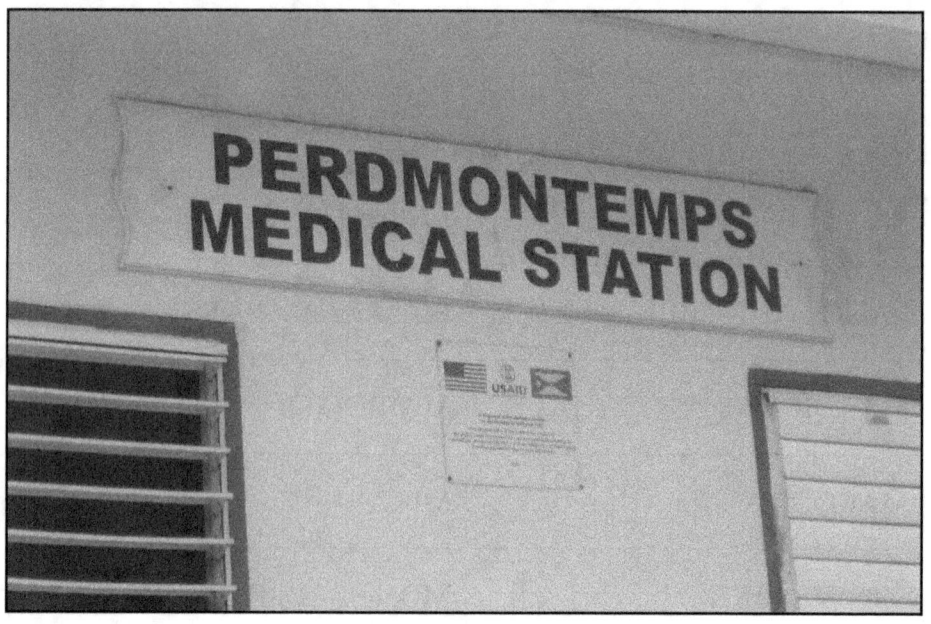

Illustration 3.4 Signage for the Perdmontemps Medical Station
Perdmontemps is a community in the parish of St. David.

PETIT BACAYE	PETIT CARENAGE (CARRIACOU)
PETIT ÉTANG	PETIT TROU
PETITE ANSE	PETITE ESPÉRANCE
PITON [HILL] (PETITE MARTINIQUE)	PLAISANCE
POINT SALINES	POMME ROSE

REQUIN [BAY]	SANS SOUCI
SAUTEURS	SOUBISE
TERRES CANNES	THÉBAÏDE
TIVOLI	TUILLERIES
VENDÔME	VINCENNES

In addition to the toponyms listed above, many small enclaves or communities in Grenada's parishes bear French-derived (or Kéyòl) names that were likely given by Grenadian monolingual Kéyòl speakers rather than by the French. A sampling of these names, taken from the parish of St. Patrick, is provided below in Kéyòl. These toponyms are not widely recorded; they are simply known to and used by the communities living in the different parishes. The Kéyòl writing system, presented later in this book, has been applied to the spelling of these place names.

BOUCHÈRI	BWAKOKO
CHAMBON	DÉKAI
DIZÉLIZ	FON
FONBOULÉ	GRIZON
GWO TANT	LADO
LANS KOTO	LASOUS
LAYVYÈ BAMBOU	MÒTÈL BA
PITI TANT	PITON
TOULOMBÈ	TOUWAVIN

4

LESSER ANTILLEAN FRENCH-LEXICON CREOLE: BASIC GRAMMAR

Historical Overview and Comparative Elements

For historical reasons, Lesser Antillean French-lexicon Creole remains a predominantly oral language. Until recently, little attention had been paid to its codification, largely because of the low socio-economic status of its speakers and the mistaken view that French-lexicon Creole was an inferior spin-off of the French language rather than a separate language in its own right.

It is no accident that many of the world's endangered languages do not exist in written form: writing a language is critical to its preservation. With the decline of Grenada's Kéyòl, Grenadians have lost some important aspects of their folklore, many of their stories, knowledge of the island's ecosystem, particularly its plant life and, in general terms, a vast repository of wisdom. Sadly, the development of the writing system of Lesser Antillean French-lexicon Creole will likely remain an uphill battle in the years ahead for two main reasons: the number of speakers is relatively small and, in all the countries where this language is spoken, it coexists with a language that enjoys international recognition or status (French, English and Spanish).

Among the first persons to attempt to document French-lexicon Creole grammar was John Jacob Thomas. Born in Trinidad in 1841, Thomas also spent some time in Grenada. In 1869, Thomas produced a pioneering work on Trinidad's French-lexicon Creole language entitled *The Theory and Practice of Creole Grammar*. This foundational work explores the orthography, etymology and syntax of the French-lexicon Creole language and reviews a number of its idioms and proverbs. Little or nothing had been documented on French-lexicon Creole during

Thomas' era and, for a long time, his book stood as the lone study of and tribute to this language. Clearly a lover of French-lexicon Creole, Thomas once described it as 'the most delightful and widely spoken' language in Trinidad during his era.

Another key contributor to the written form of French-lexicon Creole is Martiniquan Elodie Jourdain, whose doctoral thesis, *Du français aux parlers créoles*, was published posthumously in 1956. In it, she explores in great detail the phonetic and grammatical aspects of French-lexicon Creole and concludes her study with a comparison of the French-lexicon Creoles of a number of countries, including Haiti, Guadeloupe, Mauritius and Martinique.

The works written by Thomas and Jourdain provided very useful insights into my own study of the Grenadian Kéyòl language. They and those who came after them succeeded in laying a strong foundation that would inspire others to explore, codify and raise the visibility and stature of this language.

In more recent times, extensive work has been done in St. Lucia on Lesser Antillean French-lexicon grammar, and the Grenadian French-lexicon Creole orthography outlined in the pages that follow has been adapted from the St. Lucian Kwéyòl writing system. Despite the fact that Grenada's Kéyòl belongs to the Lesser Antillean French-lexicon Creole language sub-group, there are slight differences in the pronunciation (and therefore in the spelling) of some words. For example, the pronouns 'they', 'their' or 'them' are pronounced and spelled as *yo* in many islands of this sub-group but as *yé* in Grenada. In addition, in Grenadian French-lexicon Creole, the <r> is often suppressed in French-derived words that begin with <cr>, while in other islands, the <r> is pronounced as an /r/ and in others as a /w/. By way of an example, and restricting the comparison to Grenada and St. Lucia, the verb 'to call' or 'to shout' in Lesser Antillean French-lexicon Creole, lexically derived from the French verb *crier*, would be pronounced and thus written as *kiyé* in Grenada but as *kwiyé* in St. Lucia. Similarly, the French word *Créole* would be written as *Kéyòl* in Grenada but as *Kwéyòl* in St. Lucia, following the pronunciation of these words. The pronunciation of these and similar words can be heard in the third part of this work, which is composed of audio-visual recordings of Grenadian French-lexicon Creole speakers.

In French-lexicon Creole there is a very close correspondence between the spoken and written words, in part because the spelling system was developed only recently. Like the English language, the French-lexicon Creole language contains digraphs (a combination of two letters representing one sound) and trigraphs (a combination of three letters representing one sound). An example of a digraph in English is <ph> as in the word 'phenomenon'; an example of a digraph in French-lexicon Creole is <tj> as in *tjè* (heart). An example of a trigraph in English is <igh> as in the word 'sigh'; and example of a trigraph in French-lexicon Creole is <ann> as in *vann* (to sell).

Despite the lexical similarities between French-lexicon Creole and French, the grammatical rules governing these two languages are quite different. In French-lexicon Creole, as is the case with a number of other languages, a process of agglutination of French words often takes place. For example, the French definite article is often fused in French-lexicon Creole with the noun it modifies. The French *les amis* [English: the friends] therefore becomes *zami* in French-lexicon Creole, with the /s/ at the end of the definite article *les* being fused with the word *ami* to form *zami*. Similarly, the French *du thé* [English: some tea] becomes *dité* in French-lexicon Creole, as the two separate French words are merged to form one in French-lexicon Creole. Most French-lexicon Creole words that begin with <z> were therefore formed through a process of agglutination of French words. Still in the lexical sphere, the French-lexicon Creole word *gason* [English: boy] is readily recognisable as being derived from the French word *garçon*. However, the singular form of 'the boy' in French is *le garçon*, while in French-lexicon Creole it is *gason-la*. The plural form of 'the boys' in French is *les garçons*, while in French-lexicon Creole it is *sé gason-la*.

The final comment relates to verb formation in French-lexicon Creole. The verb serves as the grammatical anchor of any language. Tense formation in the French-lexicon Creole language is radically different from that in French. In French-lexicon Creole, verb tenses are indicated by markers. It should be pointed out that these markers are also present in a number of West African languages. Dr Morgan Dalphinis, a St. Lucian expert on Caribbean and African languages, explores and illustrates the grammatical connection between Creole languages and a number of West African languages in his book *Caribbean and African Languages: Social History, Language, Literature and Education*. It is also interesting to note that there are a number of striking similarities between the French-lexicon Creole of the Caribbean region in general and the French-lexicon Creole spoken by the inhabitants of a region geographically far removed from the Caribbean—the Indian Ocean Region, to which islands such as Mauritius and Reunion belong. Mauritius, a modern-day multi-ethnic island composed largely of Indo-Mauritians (persons of Indian descent), Sino-Mauritians (persons of Chinese descent) and Creoles (persons of African descent), also has a history of slavery and a French presence (1715-1810). The people brought to its shores to work on the plantations came largely from East Africa (Madagascar, Mozambique, Malawi and Zambia), with smaller numbers coming from West Africa.

In the pages that follow, the basic aspects of Lesser Antillean French-lexicon Creole grammar, adapted to Grenada, are presented. For illustrative purposes, one set of example French-lexicon Creole sentences is accompanied by its English-lexicon Creole equivalents. This chapter does not outline all the grammatical aspects of the language. The author's aim is simply to provide the reader with a fuller appreciation of the fundamental elements of this rich language, and particularly its writing system, which has been applied to the words and phrases appearing in the glossary. The oral component of Grenadian Kéyòl is presented in the video accompanying this book, which features interviews with the Grenadian speakers of the language.

Pronunciation Guide: Vowels

Oral Vowels

		English Example	**Kéyòl Example**	
a	as in	cat	chat	(cat)
è	as in	let	bèl	(nice)
é	as in	grey	balé	(broom)

i	as in	gr**ee**n	l**i**v	(pound)
ò	as in	c**o**t	lap**ò**t	(door)
o	as in	r**oa**d	ch**o**	(hot)
ou	as in	r**u**le	f**ou**	(crazy)
ay	as in	h**igh**	lak**ay**	(home)

Nasal Vowels

an	d**an**	(tooth)
en	p**en**	(bread)
on	p**on**	(bridge)

Semi-vowels

w	as in	**w**orry	**w**òm	(rum)
y	as in	**y**ou	ch**y**en	(dog)

Pronunciation Guide: Consonants

The following consonants are similar to their English equivalents (<c>, <q> and <x> are not used in Kéyòl):

b	**b**agay	(thing)
d	**d**oudou	(darling)
f	**f**am	(woman)
g	**g**adé	(look)
h	**h**ad	(clothes)
j	**j**ouvé	(the official start of carnival festivities in the very early hours of Carnival Monday)

k	**k**atolik	(Catholic)
l	**l**alin	(moon)
m	**m**ako	(nosey)
n	**n**òm	(man)
p	**p**alé	(to speak)
r	la**r**ènn	(queen)
s	**s**abo	(shoe)
t	**t**onnè	(expression of great surprise)
v	**v**ann	(to sell)
w	**w**i	(yes)
z	**z**aboka	(avocado)

The following consonant combinations (digraphs) are different from English:

ch	**ch**apo	(hat) (English would generally use <sh> as in **sh**ow)
dj	**dj**amèt	(loose, uncouth woman) (English uses <j> as in **j**ump)
tj	**tj**è	(heart) (English uses <ch> as in **ch**urch)
ng	mové la**ng**	(to gossip maliciously)

The following vowel-consonant combinations (trigraphs) also exist:

enn	j**enn** (young)
ann	v**ann** (sell)
onn	y**onn** (one)

Personal Pronouns

Subject Pronouns

mwen/mon	I
ou	you (singular)
i, li	he, she, it
nou	we
zò	you (plural)
yé	they

Examples

Grenadian French-lexicon Creole	**English**
Mwen sé yon dòktè.	I am a doctor.
Éti **ou** ka alé?	Where are you going?
I sé mama-mwen.	She is my mother.
Nou ka wété Lagwinad.	We live in Grenada.
Zò sòt.	You (plural) are silly.
Yé pa konnèt ki moun **nou** yé.	They don't know who we are.

Object Pronouns

mwen/mon	me
ou	you (singular)
i, li	him, her, it
nou	us
zò	you (plural)
yé	them

Examples

Grenadian French-lexicon Creole — Grenadian English-lexicon Creole

Grenadian French-lexicon Creole	Grenadian English-lexicon Creole
Si ou sé nòm, ba **mwen**.	If you is man, hit me.
Vini! Mwen pa pè **ou**.	Come! I in fraid you.
Kiyé **i** ba mwen.	Call him give me.
I méné yon bawi pou **nou**.	She send a barrel for us.
I kay jouwé **zò**, wi.	She go cuss all you, *wi*.
Mwen pa ka palé épi **yé**.	I in talkin to them.

The Possessive

The personal pronoun (*mwen*, *ou*, etc.) is used as a possessive marker. It is placed after the noun to which the possessive applies.

Examples

Grenadian French-lexicon Creole	English
gangang-**mwen**	my grandmother
lékòl-**ou**	your school
lakay-**li**	his/her home
mama-**nou**	our mother
zyé-**zò**	your (plural) eyes
had-**yé**	their clothes

Articles

Definite Article

The definite article ('the') is placed <u>after</u> the noun to which it refers. For example, *fam-la* means 'the woman'. There are two forms of the definite article, depending on the final sound of the noun.

'**-a**' if the word ends in a vowel sound

Examples

Grenadian French-lexicon Creole	**English**
tifi-a	the girl
lamowi-a	the saltfish
misyé-a	the man
lawi-a	the street
diwi-a	the rice

'**-la**' if the word does not end in a vowel sound

Examples

Grenadian French-lexicon Creole	**English**
bagay-la	the thing
nòm-la	the man
jaden-la	the garden
pip-la	the pipe
mouskad-la	the nutmeg

Indefinite Article

The indefinite article ('a' or 'an') is formed by placing *yon* or *on* (used interchangeably) <u>before</u> the noun to which it refers.

Examples

Grenadian French-lexicon Creole — English

yon misyé	a man
yon kanòt	a boat
yon latjé	a tail
yon pyé	a foot
yon jou	a day

Verb Tenses

Verb tenses are indicated by auxiliary words or markers that precede the verb. The verb remains unchanged; the marker or auxiliary word changes to denote the tense.

Present Tense

The present tense is formed by placing the marker *ka* before the verb.

Verb – palé	**to speak**
mwen **ka** palé	I speak/I am speaking
ou **ka** palé	you speak/you are speaking
i, li **ka** palé	he/she speaks/he/she is speaking
nou **ka** palé	we speak/we are speaking
zò **ka** palé	you (plural) speak/you (plural) are speaking
yé **ka** palé	they are speaking

Examples

Grenadian French-lexicon Creole — English

I **ka** fimé pip-li.	She is smoking her pipe.
Yé **ka** wamasé mouskad toulé jou.	They pick up nutmegs every day.

Simple Past Tense

The simple past tense is formed by using the verb in its unmarked form.

mwen palé	I spoke
ou palé	you spoke
i, li palé	he/she spoke
nou palé	we spoke
zò palé	you (plural) spoke
yé palé	they spoke

Examples

Grenadian French-lexicon Creole	**English**
Mwen tombé, mwen pa mouwi.	I fell (but) I did not die.
Mwen alé Labé.	I went to Grenville.

Pluperfect Tense

The pluperfect tense is formed by placing the marker *té* before the verb.

mwen **té** palé	I had spoken
ou **té** palé	you had spoken
i, li **té** palé	he/she had spoken
nou **té** palé	we had spoken
zò **té** palé	you (plural) had spoken
yé **té** palé	they had spoken

Examples

Grenadian French-lexicon Creole   English

Lè mwen wivé, tout moun **té** manjé.   When I arrived, everyone had eaten.

Lè mwen gadé, i **té** jambé layvyè-a.   When I looked, she had crossed the river.

Imperfect Tense

The imperfect tense is formed by placing the markers *té ka* before the verb

mwen **té ka** palé	I used to speak/I was speaking
ou **té ka** palé	you used to speak/you were speaking
i, li **té ka** palé	he/she used to speak/he/she was speaking
nou **té ka** palé	we used to speak/we were speaking
zò **té ka** palé	you (plural) used to speak/you (plural) were speaking
yé **té ka** palé	they used to speak/they were speaking

Examples

Grenadian French-lexicon Creole   English

Bouden-gangang **té ka** fè i mal.   Granny's belly used to hurt her.

Mwen **té ka** lavé lè i vini.   I was washing when she came.

Immediate Future Tense

The immediate future tense is formed by placing the markers *ka alé* before the verb.

mwen **ka alé** palé   I am going to speak

ou **ka alé** palé	you are going to speak
i, li **ka alé** palé	he/she is going to speak
nou **ka alé** palé	we are going to speak
zò **ka alé** palé	you (plural) are going to speak
yé **ka alé** palé	they are going to speak

Examples

Grenadian French-lexicon Creole	**English**
I **ka alé** bouwi manjé.	She is going to cook.
Yé **ka alé** lavé nan layvyè-a.	They are going to wash in the river.

Simple Future Tense

The simple future tense is formed by placing the marker *kay* before the verb.

mwen **kay** palé	I will speak
ou **kay** palé	you will speak
i, li **kay** palé	he/she will speak
nou **kay** palé	we will speak
zò **kay** palé	you (plural) will speak
yé **kay** palé	they will speak

Examples

Grenadian French-lexicon Creole	**English**
Mwen **kay** ba ou yann.	I will give you licks.
Mwen **kay** mò lafen.	I will die of hunger.
Soukouyan **kay** sousé san-ou.	Soukouyan will suck your

MWEN KA ALÉ

blood.

Numbers

0-zéwo, nòt	**11**- onz	**22**- ven-dé
1-yonn	**12**- douz	**30**- twant
2-dé	**13**- twèz	**40**- kawant
3-twa	**14**- katòz	**50**- senkant
4-kat	**15**- kenz	**60**- swasant
5-senk	**16**- sèz	**70**- sèptant
6-sis	**17**- dizsèt	**80**- oktant/katwiven
7-sèt	**18**- dizswit	**90**- nwanant
8-wit	**19**- dizsnèf	**1000**- mil
9-nèf	**20**- ven	
10-dis	**21**- vent-é-yonn	

Days of the Week

dimanch	Sunday
lendi	Monday
madi	Tuesday
mèkwédi	Wednesday
jédi	Thursday
vandwédi	Friday

samdi	Saturday

Months of the Year

janvyé	January
févwiyé	February
mas	March
awvi	April
mé	May
jwen	June
jwiyé	July
out	August
sèptam	September
òktòb	October
novam	November
désam	December

5

KÉYÒL RETENTIONS IN GRENADIAN ENGLISH-LEXICON CREOLE: GLOSSARY OF WORDS AND PHRASES

Caribbean people express themselves in ways that are by turns concise, rich and figurative. As a lover of language and languages in general, my deepest love and passion have always been for my own Grenadian English-lexicon Creole, for it is the only language that allows me to delve deep within and convey my thoughts cogently and clearly in instances where Standard English falls short or simply misses the mark.

To illustrate Grenadians' expressive way of speaking, I chose to start the second part of this work—a glossary dedicated to the French-lexicon words and phrases used in Grenadian English-lexicon Creole—with a short poem to illustrate how Grenadian speech, rich with metaphors and hyperbole, is influenced by the island's French-lexicon Creole.

<u>Mèm Bagay</u>

I did hear a voice that sound like Annette

So I decide to go outside and rèkonnèt

In the yard was one set a bakanal

Between she and the neighbour, makmè Percival

I hear him say: 'you is a old wajang;

They should call you queen mové lang'

MWEN KA ALÉ

She say: 'And you is a mamapoul

But you tryin to behave like a mad bull

If you touch me, I givin you one planas

That go teach you not to be so damn farse'

He shout back: 'Let me tell you something miss mako

I kickin you tail straight in the cocoa'

Old Miss Mary chime in: 'I tired of this komès

All you two creatin too much stress

Stop actin like all you modi

And you, Annette, behave like a lady

Forget about what is true and what is lie,

Keeper and woman, that is mèm bagay'.

Notes on the Glossary

1. For historical and linguistic reasons, it should be pointed out that the French settlers who first established colonies in the Caribbean in the 1600s generally hailed from the northern regions of France, including Normandy (*la Normandie*), Picardy (*la Picardie*) and Brittany (*la Bretagne*). Consequently, the French words or vocabulary appearing in this glossary could, in some instances, reflect certain French regionalisms and, in others, archaic French. By way of illustration, the French-lexicon Creole verb *ba* is derived from the archaic French verb *bailler* (to give).

2. In Grenadian English-lexicon Creole, lexical reduplication, defined as the intentional replication of part of a word or an

entire word to form a new word, is very common in everyday speech. Lexical reduplication serves the grammatical function of emphasis or intensification. For those familiar with Grenada, think, for example, of how often one hears expressions like 'I get vex, vex' in Grenadian English-lexicon Creole. This phenomenon is a common feature of a number of West African languages that has been retained in Creole languages, regardless of lexical influence. The Kéyòl glossary that follows also contains examples of lexical reduplication in such words as *dou-dou* (darling) and *touf-touf* (someone of short stature and heavy build).

3. The common Kéyòl names of plants and fruits have been provided, along with their scientific names, where available. None of the information in the glossary pertaining to the use of plants, herbs, trees and grasses in traditional medicine in Grenada is intended to be used for any medicinal purpose whatsoever. The information has been provided for the sole purpose of giving the reader a full appreciation of Grenada's culture and history and should therefore not be construed as an explicit or implicit claim or recommendation by the author that these are effective in treating or curing any illness or medical condition.

4. All definitions appearing in the glossary are specific to Grenada. Semantic shifts in words from one French-lexicon-Creole-speaking country to another are therefore possible, even within the sub-group of Lesser Antillean Creole-speaking countries.

5. The glossary contains only those Kéyòl terms for which a clear or likely link to the French language could be established by the author. Consequently, terms that appear to belong to Grenada's French-lexicon Creole but could not be linked to the French language were excluded. While every effort has been made to verify the accuracy of the entries appearing in the glossary, there may be instances of omissions or errors or cases where fuller or clearer explanations are required. The author welcomes feedback that could be incorporated into a revised edition of this work. The following email address may be used to contact the author: rlagrenade@gmail.com.

Format of Glossary Entries

1. Kéyòl word (in bold)

2. Part of speech (as used in Kéyòl)

3. Etymology ('prob' before a term indicates possible or likely, but not definitive, etymology).

4. Definition (English equivalent and/or explanation)

5. A sentence illustrating use of the word/phrase in Grenadian English-lexicon Creole (where necessary)

6. A Standard English equivalent of the Grenadian English-lexicon Creole sentence

7. Other useful information

The following abbreviations have been used:

adj	adjective
adv	adverb
adv excl	adverbial exclamation
excl	exclamation
excl phr	exclamatory phrase
exp	expression
Fr	French
imp vb	imperative verb
int	interrogative
interj	interjection
int pr	interrogative pronoun
n	noun

phr	phrase
pr	pronoun
prob	probably
vb	verb
vulg	vulgar

Grenadian Kéyòl Glossary

abatwa n [<Fr *abattoir*]/slaughterhouse. Grenada's *abatwa* is located on Melville Street, in the island's capital, St. George's.

afòs adv excl [<Fr *à force [de]*]/by dint of. Used as an adverbial intensifier to introduce the idea of 'how', 'so much' or 'to such an extent'. E.g., *Afòs* it does kill them when they see how nice my yard look! [**How it kills them when they see how nice my yard looks!**]

anmwen interj [<Fr *à moi!*]/help! Once used as a call of distress or a call for help during stick fighting (see *kalinda*). The term continues to be used in Grenadian English-lexicon Creole to convey an extreme reaction. E.g., When I hear the news, I had to bawl *anmwen*! [**When I heard the news, I uttered a cry for help.**]

babalé n [<Fr *barbe à lait*]/milk beard. A hot drink made of soursop, milk, sugar and water.

bagas n [<Fr *bagasse*]/bagasse. A fibrous residue obtained after sugar cane stalks are crushed.

Illustration 5.1
The sugar cane plant (*Saccharum officinarum*)
The sugar cane plant, from which bagas is obtained.

bakanal n [<Fr *bacchanale*]/drunken revelry (associated with carnival in the Caribbean). Outside of the carnival context, the term may also refer to confusion and discord.

balé dou n [<Fr *balai doux*]/sweet broom. A flowering plant used in traditional medicine to treat a variety of ailments, including diabetes and colds. Scientific name: *Scoparia dulcis*.

balé kay n [<Fr *balai [la] case*]/hut broom. The branches of this tree are sometimes used to sweep homes in Grenada. The Kéyòl word *kay* means 'home'.

balé lakou n [<Fr *balai la cour*]/yard broom.

balé mindi n [<Fr *balai*]/broom + [<Fr *midi*]/noon, midday. In traditional medicine in Grenada, this plant is considered to have antifungal properties. Scientific name: *Sida acuta*.

balijé n [<Fr *balisier*]/canna. A popular tropical plant in Grenada and the Caribbean in general. There are several varieties of the *balijé* plant, which resembles the banana plant and bears strikingly beautiful reddish-orange flowers. The term *balijé* is the symbol of political parties in Trinidad and Martinique. Scientific name: *Heliconia bihai*.

bazodi adj [<Fr *abasourdi*]/stunned. In Grenada, the term *bazodi* means 'dazed' or 'confused'.

bèbè n [<Fr *bébé*]/baby. A foolish person.

bèlè n [prob <Fr *bel air*]. The French term *bel air* means 'attractive' or 'appealing'; the Kéyòl term *bèlè* refers to a folk dance once common in Grenada and still popular in St. Lucia and Dominica.

bètouj n [<Fr *bête rouge*]/red beast. In Grenada, *bètouj* is a red ant that stings.

bidé n [<Fr *bidet*]/bidet. A plumbing fixture used for washing the genitalia.

bodwi anglé n [<Fr *broderie anglaise*]/English embroidery. Clothing that features a needlework technique with oval holes and fine stitching

around these holes to form various patterns. Once done by hand, this embroidery is now done by machines.

bomviwé n [<Fr *bon*]/good + [<Fr *virer*]/ turn around. A quick, witty comeback or repartee.

bondjé excl phr [<Fr *bon dieu*]. Literally 'good God'. E.g., *Bondjé* child, stop runnin. You go fall! [**Good God, child, stop running. You will fall!**]

bondjé béni mwen phr [<Fr *bon dieu* + *bénir* + *moi*]. Expression used as a pledge or vow to indicate that one is speaking the truth. Roughly equivalent to 'so help me God!'

bonjou n [<Fr *bonjour*]/good morning, good day.

bonswè n [<Fr *bonsoir*]/good evening.

bosi adj [<Fr *bossu*]/hunchbacked. E.g., A ole *bosi*-back woman. [**An old hunchbacked woman.**]

bou-bou n [prob <Fr *bobo*]/scratch, cut.

bouché n [<Fr *bouchée*]/mouthful. In Grenada, the term refers to a very small pastry filled with fish or meat and eaten as a hors d'oeuvre.

bouchèt n [<Fr *bréchet*]/breastbone or sternum. In traditional medicine, a fallen *bouchèt* is thought to create a host of stomach and other ailments.

bouden milé n [<Fr *boudin*]/black pudding + [<Fr *mulet*]/mule. The Kéyòl term *bouden* also means 'belly'. *Bouden milé* refers to a plant used in traditional medicine as a cleanser.

bouf n [prob <Fr *bouffée*]. The Kéyòl term is perhaps linked to the French term *bouffée*, meaning outburst. The term is used in Grenada to mean an insult or reprimand.

bouj n [<Fr *bourgeois*]. Someone perceived to be affluent and/or occupying the upper echelons of the social strata.

brazyé n [<Fr *brassière*]/bra, brassiere.

bwa bandé n [<Fr *bois bandé*]. The French term *bois* means 'wood' and *bander* means 'to have an erection'. *Bwa bandé* refers to a tree in Grenada whose bark and leaves are used as an aphrodisiac. Scientific name: *Chione venosa*.

bwa blan n [<Fr *bois blanc*]/white wood. A tree that bears a fragrant white flower. Scientific name: *Symplocos martinicensis*.

bwa bouk n [<Fr *bois bouc*]. Literally 'goat wood', the term refers to a type of tree the stiff branches of which are tied together to make a yard broom.

Illustration 5.2 A broom made from the *bwa bouk* tree
These brooms are used for sweeping yards in Grenada.

bwa-bwa n [<Fr *bois*]. From the French term for wood (reduplicated), *bwa-bwa* refers to a carnival character who parades through the streets on wooden stilts wearing a colourful costume. He is similar to the *moko jumbie* carnival character. See Folk Songs, Carnival and Calypso above.

bwadenn n [<Fr *bois d'inde*]/India wood. Also known as the bay leaf tree, this tree is very common in Grenada and many other Caribbean islands. The tree's leaves are used to make bay rum and bay oil. Scientific name: *Pimenta racemosa.*

bwa fè n [<Fr *bois [de] fer*]. Literally 'iron wood', the term refers to a type of tree in Grenada with very strong branches. The wood from this tree is used to make charcoal and as supporting pillars in the construction of wooden houses. This wood was also once used to make sticks for *kalinda* stick fights.

bwa flo n [<Fr *bois*]/wood + [*flo*]. There are two possible origins of the word *flo*—the West African Fulani language, in which the term *floflo* means 'hollow', and the French language in which the word *flot* means 'afloat' (<Fr *être à flot*/to be afloat). The Kéyòl term *bwa flo* refers to a tree whose leaves are similar to those of the *bwa kano* tree. The *bwa flo* tree grows quickly and its wood is very lightweight and can be used as a substitute for cork. Scientific name: *Ochroma pyramidale.*

bwa gouti n [<Fr *bois*]/wood + [*agouti*]. A tree endemic to Grenada. Scientific name: *Maytenus grenadensis.* The term 'agouti', of indigenous origin, refers to a rodent eaten in Grenada.

bwa gri n [<Fr *bois gris*]/grey wood. A species of forest timber. Scientific name: *Licania ternatensis.*

bwa kabwit n [<Fr *bois cabri*]/goat wood. Branches of this shrub are used to sweep yards. (Strictly speaking, the French term *cabri* refers to a kid, while the Kéyòl term *kabwit* refers to a kid or goat.)

bwa kano n [<Fr *bois canon*]/cannon wood. A tree with hollow branches and large leaves. The appearance of the tree changes depending on weather conditions. The leaves of this tree were sometimes used

in Grenada as a substitute for tobacco. Scientific name: *Cecropia schreberiana.*

Illustration 5.3 The *bwa kano* tree (*Cecropia schreberiana*)
The leaves of this tree signal the onset of weather disturbances by turning greyish-green and folding inward.

bwa lé   n [<Fr *bois lait*]/milk wood. A small tree that bears white flowers. Scientific name: *Rauvolfia nitida.*

bwa pini   n [<Fr *bois*]/wood + [<Fr *punir*]/punish. A tree with conal-shaped bumps on the trunk. Scientific name: *Zanthoxylum martinicense.*

bwa sèk   n [<Fr *bois sec*]. The French term translates as 'dry wood'. The term *bwa sèk* is used in storytelling in Grenada and other Caribbean territories. Stories are narrated in a call-and-response format. To signal the start of the story, the storyteller says *tim tim*, and the audience responds *bwa sèk*. With these opening words, the story or riddle begins. While the etymology is French, the storytelling practice is African.

bwa wouj n [<Fr *bois rouge*]/red wood. A species in the mahogany family. Scientific name: *Guarea macrophyla.*

bwa zòm n [<Fr *bois d'orme*]/elm wood]. A tree found in the mountainous areas of Grenada. Scientific name: *Guazuma ulmifolia.*

chaben n [<Fr *chabin*]. The French term *chabin* refers to a hybrid or cross between a sheep and a goat. In Grenada, the term is used metaphorically to refer to a light-skinned person of African ancestry.

chado béni n [<Fr *chardon béni*]/blessed thistle. This herb, similar to cilantro (coriander), is used as a spice in foods and to treat colds in traditional medicine. Scientific name: *Eryngium foetidum.*

Illustration 5.4 The *chado béni* plant (*Eryngium foetidum*)
The pungent leaves of this plant are used as a culinary spice and in traditional medicine.

chandinèl kléwé n [<Fr *chandelle éclairée*]/lighted candle. The name of a song once commonly sung at wakes (see definition of *lakampayn*) in Grenada. (See video **Chapter 2: Religious and Spiritual Expression**; *Lakampayn (Prayer for the Deceased): Discussion and Songs* video clip.)

chantwèl n [<Fr *chanterelle*]/the e-string of the violin. The term *chantwèl* is used in the context of Grenada's short-knee masqueraders (see Folksongs, Carnival and Calypso above) and Carriacou Big Drum dancing to refer to the lead singer or soloist.

chaplé n [<Fr *chapelet*]/rosary.

chapo glo n [<Fr *chapeau de l'eau*]/water hat. A low-lying plant that grows near the water. Its broad leaves are sometimes tied to the forehead to treat headaches. Scientific name: *Lepianthes peltata*.

chatennyé n [<Fr *chataignier*]/chestnut tree. A very tall tree found in Grenada's rain forest. Scientific name: *Sloanea caribaea*.

chimiz n [<Fr *chemise*]/shirt.

chofè n [<Fr *chauffeur*]/driver.

chou-chou v [<Fr *chuchoter*]/to whisper. To speak in a low voice, often in the context of gossiping. E.g., You think I in hear all you *chou-chouin* outside? I know is me all you was talkin about! [**You think I didn't hear you whispering outside? I know you were talking about me!**]

dachin n [<Fr *chou de chine*] (Allsopp 2003, 188)/ Chinese cabbage. Dasheen is a tuber widely eaten in soups and as a steamed vegetable in Grenada.

dèch adj [<Fr *dèche*]/abject poverty. The Kéyòl term *dèch* is used in Grenada to refer to someone who is naïve or gullible.

déchéché adj [<Fr *déchiré*]/torn up, trashed.

dégoflé n [<Fr *dégonfler*]/to let air out. The leaves of this plant are boiled and drunk to help pass gas. Also known as *wajé pété* (see definition). Scientific name: *Hyptis capitata*.

démélé adj [<Fr *démêlé*]. From the French verb *démêler* (to disentangle), the Kéyòl term *démélé* in Grenada is used to refer to the ability to get oneself out of a tight spot or difficult situation. E.g., Is livin in America that teach me how to *démélé* myself. [**Life in America taught me how to get myself out of tricky situations.**]

dimanch gwa n [<Fr *dimanche gras*]. Literally translated as 'fat Sunday', the term *dimanch gwa* refers to the Sunday preceding Lent (or Shrove Sunday) that marks the high point of carnival. The term *gras* (fat) refers to the eating of meat that precedes the Lenten season. During this season, some Christians fast and abstain from the consumption of meat.

dimijan n [<Fr *dame-jeanne*]/demijohn. A narrow-necked bottle, encased in wicker, once used for storing water in Grenada. The design of this bottle helps keep the water it contains cool.

dingolé adj [<Fr *dégringolé*]. Derived from the French verb '*dégringoler*', meaning 'to tumble down', the term is used in Grenada in exactly the same sense but often in the narrower context of carnival dancing and festivities.

dité péyi n [<Fr *du thé [du] pays*]/the country's tea. A plant used in traditional medicine to treat a variety of ailments, including eye infections. Scientific name: *Capraria biflora*.

Illustration 5.5 The *dité péyi* plant (*Capraria biflora*)
This plant is thought to have anti-bacterial properties
and is used to treat eye infections.

djab djab n [<Fr *diable*]. From the French word for 'devil', the reduplicative Kéyòl term *djab djab* is used exclusively in a carnival context to refer to masqueraders who assume a devil-like appearance by painting their skin black, wearing horns attached to an inverted chamber pot, and sometimes carrying large snakes around their necks. *Djab djabs* masquerade on *jouvé* (see definition) morning. (See section on Folk Songs, Carnival and Calypso above).

djalousi n [<Fr *jalousie*]. This term, the French for 'venetian blind', refers to wooden shutters once common in homes in Grenada.

djamèt n [<Fr *diamètre*]/diameter. The term is derived from the dividing lines between the different social strata, with a *djamèt* coming from the lower echelons of society. The term *djamèt* generally refers to a coarse, loud woman.

djasmin sovaj n [<Fr *jasmine sauvage*]/wild jasmine. Used in traditional medicine in Grenada to treat a variety of ailments. Scientific name: *Cestrum latifolium.*

djènè adj [<Fr *gêné*]/embarrassed.

djèri-tout n [<Fr *guérir tout*]/cure-all. A very popular traditional medicine plant. Scientific name: *Pluchea carolinensis.*

djouk jodi adv [<Fr *jusqu'à aujourd'hui*]. From the French term meaning 'until now', the Kéyòl term *djouk jodi* is used to refer to an event that was supposed to happen and never did or a promise that was made and never kept. E.g., Since last year he promise to pay me the money he owe me. *Djouk jodi, wi.* I waitin still. [**Since last year he promised to repay the money he owes me. Up to now, I'm still waiting.**]

djoukoutou adj [<Fr *jusqu'à vous*]. (Allsopp 2003, 316) From the French term meaning 'even you'. The 'you' in the Kéyòl term conveys the sense of someone insignificant or unimportant. E.g., Ay, Ay, *djoukoutou* Mary and all runnin she mouth on me! [**Even insignificant Mary is gossiping about me!**]

do do piti popo phr [<Fr *dodo petite poupée*]/sleep little doll. The title of a Kéyòl lullaby in Grenada, which translates as 'sleep little baby'.

The lyrics of the song are quite terrifying—the message of the lullaby is that if babies do not fall sleep, a 'Tom cat' (male cat) will eat them. (See video **Chapter 3: Folk Songs;** *Dodo Piti Popo video clip.*)

dou-dou   adj [<Fr *doux*]/sweet. The reduplicative Kéyòl term *dou-dou* is used to convey affection; it is roughly equivalent to 'darling'.

drivé   adj [<Fr *dérivé*]. From the French verb *dériver* (to be adrift), the Kéyòl term *drivé* means 'to wander around with no sense of purpose' or 'to be out for a long period without pursuing any specific activity'. E.g., Girl I lookin for you whole mornin! You went and *drivé*? [**Girl, I've been looking for you all morning. Were you knocking about?**]

embètè   v [<Fr *embêter*]/to annoy or bother. In Grenada, the Kéyòl term *embètè* has two meanings—first, 'to irritate' or 'to bother' and second, when used as an adjective, to describe someone perceived as stupid or unintelligent.

è mwen wi   excl phr [Eh] + [<Fr *moi oui*]. A phrase used to express surprise or disbelief. E.g., The child beat he father last week. *È mwen wi*! What this world comin to? [**The child struck his father last week. Good heavens! What is the world coming to?**]

falèz   n [<Fr *falaise*]/cliff. The name of an area with a very steep cliff in the Grand Anse area of Grenada. The word *falèz* is sometimes mispronounced, through a process of incorrect refinement, as 'fall edge'.

farin   n [<Fr *farine*]/flour. In Grenada, *farin* refers specifically to manioc flour (the substance that remains after the cassava juice has been extracted). After preparation, the finished product (*farin*) resembles a coarse, grainy powder.

fenni   adj [<Fr *fané*]/withered. Term used to describe a person with a deformed body part. E.g., He have a *fenni* hand. [**He has a malformed hand.**]

fèt   n [<Fr *fête*]/party.

flakoché   n [<Fr *flacourtie*]/flacourtia. A fruit more commonly known in Grenada as governor's plum. Produced by a tree with a

sometimes spiny bark, the fruit becomes dark red or purple when ripe. The term 'flacourtia' is derived from Etienne de Flacourt, the Director of the French East India Company who led an expedition to Madagascar in the mid-1600s. Scientific name: *Flacourtia jangomas*.

Illustration 5.6 The *flakoché* fruit (*Flacourtia jangomas*)
This is also known in Grenada as governor's plum.

flambo   n [<Fr *flambeau*]/torch. An outdoor lamp or torch made by partially filling an empty bottle with kerosene and stuffing the opening of the bottle with pieces of fabric and lighting it.

flanè v [<Fr *flâner*]. From the French verb meaning 'to stroll', the term *flanè* in Grenadian Kéyòl has more or less the same meaning, but with a hint of showing off, particularly of one's clothes.

fraka n [<Fr *fracas*]/a ruckus, a scene. E.g., These people better don't fret me otherwise I makin one fraka! [**These people had better not annoy me; otherwise I'll make a scene!**]

fwè n [<Fr *frère*]/brother.

fwédi n [<Fr *froidure*]. From the French term referring to very cold weather, the Kéyòl term refers to a cold brought on by exposure to the elements. The term is also used to refer to arthritis.

gadé mizè-mwen non excl phr [<Fr *regarder* + *misère* + *moi* + *non*]. Heard more often in Grenada presently is the English-lexicon Creole equivalent of this expression 'look at my trouble, *non*!' This expression is used to express shock or disbelief.

galé adj [<Fr *galeux*]/scabby, mangy. Used (pejoratively) to describe someone whose skin is rashy or has been marked by skin disease. E.g., Watch her passin with she old *galé* foot! [**Look at her going by with her pockmarked feet!**]

gason excl [<Fr *garçon*]/boy. Used in an exclamatory manner to convey one's admiration for something.

gaté vb [<Fr *gratter*]/to scratch, to itch.

gatéwas adj [prob <Fr *gratter*]/to scratch + [<Fr *ras*]/short. A child of very short stature.

genn anba fèy n [<Fr *graine en bas feuille*]/seed-under-leaf. Known by both its Kéyòl and English names, this plant is used to treat a variety of ailments in traditional medicine in Grenada, including diabetes. The plant has been given this name because of the tiny seeds found under its leaves. Scientific name: *Phyllanthus amarus*.

Illustration 5.7 The *genn anba fèy* plant (*Phyllanthus amarus*)
Also known as seed-under-leaf.

genn égliz   n [<Fr *graine de l'église*]/church bead. A plant that produces distinctive red and black beads now used to make jewellery and once used to make rosaries. The leaves of this plant are used to treat

colds in traditional medicine in Grenada. Also known as 'jumbie bead'. Scientific name: *Abrus precatorius*.

gomyé blan   n [<Fr *gommier blanc*]/white gum tree. The wood of this tree is used to build boats. Scientific name: *Dacryodes excelsa*.

gomyé wouj   n [<Fr *gommier rouge*]/red gum tree. The wood of this tree is used to make carvings as well as posts for fences. Scientific name: *Bursera simaruba*.

gospo   n [<Fr *grosse peau*]/thick skin. The term refers to a type of citrus fruit generally used to make juices in Grenada. Also known as 'Seville orange'.

grand charge adj [<Fr *grand*]/big + [<Fr *charger*]/to charge at, to attack. A display of bravado or bluster.

grap   n [<Fr *grappe*]/cluster. Generally used in the context of fruits in Grenada. E.g., A *grap* of mangoes/coconuts. [**A cluster of mangoes/coconuts.**]

grènè   adj [<Fr *grené*]/grainy. Term used (pejoratively) to describe coarse hair. Also used to describe anything scant and grainy in appearance.

gro Michèl   n [<Fr *gros Michel*]. This term, which translates as 'big Michael', refers to a species of banana prized for its light, fluffy texture.

halé kò-ou la exp [<Fr *haler* + *corps* + *là*]. Derived from the French words *haler* meaning 'to pull' or 'to haul' and *corps* meaning 'body', the Kéyòl expression means 'move from there'.

hototo   adj [prob <Fr *haut haut haut*]. Term probably derived from the word 'high' in French (*haut*), with reduplication. This image behind this term is perhaps a roadside or market setting, where fruits and vegetables for sale are displayed in high piles or heaps. The term is generally used in a food or cooking context to mean too much of something or the overly liberal use of an ingredient. E.g., How you sharin this food *hototo* so? Everybody wouldn't get! [**Why are you serving the food so liberally? There won't be enough for everyone!**]

jan halé n [<Fr *gens* + *haler*]. From the combination of the French words *gens* (people) and *haler* (pull), the term is used in a fishing context in Grenada to refer to the members of a community who go to beaches to help fishermen pull in their nets. Usually payment for such services is in kind—persons who provide this assistance often go to the beach with a bag or calabash (from the *boli* tree) to receive their payment in the form of fish from the catch.

jo bouyà n [<Fr *l'eau bouillante*]/boiling water. A reference to sulphur springs found in different parts of Grenada and a reminder of the island's volcanic origins. People swim and relax in the warm water of these sulphur springs.

jouvé n [<Fr *jour ouvert*]. From the French term meaning 'daybreak', the term *jouvé* is associated with Carnival Monday, the first of two consecutive days of the main carnival festivities. *Jouvé* is typically the 'ole mas' day. In Grenada, the festivities begin around 5 a.m., often with the blowing of conch shells to mark the start of the festivities.

kabiyé n [<Fr *crabier*]/(crab-eating) heron.

kabiyé nwè n [<Fr *crabier noir*]/black (crab-eating) heron (Allsopp 2003, 335). Generally called a 'black bird' in Grenada.

kabousé adj [<Fr *cabossé*]/dented. The Kéyòl term is generally used in a broader sense to refer to anything that appears to be damaged extensively.

kadans n [<Fr *cadence*]/rhythm. A musical genre popular in the 1970s and 1980s in Dominica and a number of other Caribbean islands.

kadjam n [<Fr *grappe jambe*]/leg cluster. The Kéyòl term *kadjam* refers to a person's calves. E.g., Girl how you *kadjam* so hard? [**Girl why are your calves so tough?**]

kagou adj The term *kagou* refers to someone who is listless, lacking energy, or feeling vaguely unwell. The term appears to have two possible origins. First, the French term *cagoule,* referring to a penitent's hood. In the context of Roman Catholicism, this hood is worn by confraternities of penitents and generally covers the eyes and face. Second, the French term *cagot*, meaning 'sanctimonious'. (Allsopp 2003; 324) Interestingly, although the etymology of *kagou* has not been definitively established, the term is widely used and retains basically the same meaning not only in Lesser Antillean French-lexicon-Creole-speaking countries, but also in other places where French-lexicon Creole is spoken, such as Haiti and the U.S. state of Louisiana.

kaka n vulg [<Fr *caca*]/faeces.

kaka-bawi n [<Fr *caca*]/faeces + [<Fr *barré*]/striped. A large, striped fish known for its scavenging habits.

kaka-bèf n vulg [<Fr *caca*]/faeces + [<Fr *boeuf*]/cow.

kaka-béké n vulg [<Fr *caca*]/faeces + *béké*/white man. The Kéyòl word *kaka* means 'faeces' and the word *béké* is derived from the West African Igbo language, in which it refers to a white person. In Grenada and many other Caribbean islands, a *béké* refers to a light-skinned person. The *kaka-béké* plant is widely used in traditional medicine to treat eczema. Its leaves are crushed and put in bath water. Scientific name: *Senna alata*.

kaka-dan n vulg [<Fr *caca* + *dents*]. Literally 'teeth faeces', the term is used to refer to bits of food stuck in one's teeth after a meal.

kaka-djab n vulg [<Fr *caca* + *diable*]/devil's faeces. The Kéyòl term *kaka-djab* refers to a plant with a pungent odour and bitter taste that was once mixed with rum to treat stomach aches and is considered to have other medicinal properties. Asafoetida, once dispensed in pharmacies in Grenada, is derived from the resin of this plant. Scientific name: *Ferula asafoetida*.

kaka-djé n vulg [<Fr *caca* + *yeux*]. Literally 'eye faeces', the term *kaka-djé* refers to mucus found in the corner of the eyes, generally after awakening from a night's sleep.

kaka-do n vulg [<Fr *caca d'eau*]/water faeces. A dark-shelled freshwater crustacean found in shallow waters and under stones in rivers.

kaka-hole n vulg [<Fr *caca*]/faeces + [hole]. Vulgar term used to refer to the anus.

kaka-kabwit n vulg [<Fr *caca* + *cabri*]. From the French words meaning 'goat's faeces', *kaka-kabwit* is used pejoratively in Grenada to describe coarse hair that is naturally tightly rolled.

kaka-koko n vulg [<*Fr caca* + *coco*]/coconut faeces. The dark bits of coconut that remain when coconut oil is made.

kaka-né n vulg [<Fr *caca* + *nez*]/nose faeces. Mucus in the cavity of the nose.

kaka-poule n vulg [<Fr *caca* + *poule*]/fowl faeces. Also refers to a rainforest tree that bears white flowers. This tree is sometimes called *bwa sitwon* (citrus wood). Scientific name: *Ilex sideroxyloides*.

kaka-zowey n vulg [<Fr *caca* + *oreilles*]. Literally translated as 'ear faeces', the Kéyòl term is used to refer to earwax.

kampèch n [<Fr c*ampêche*]/campeachy wood (logwood). An extract of this wood is used as an astringent or antiseptic in traditional medicine. It can also be used as a dye. Scientific name: *Haematoxylum campechianum*.

kanboulé n [<Fr *cannes brûlées*]/burnt cane. The term is associated with the era of slavery, when cane fields were burned either to prepare them for harvesting or intentionally by the enslaved as an act of rebellion. In Grenada and even more so in Trinidad, the term *kanboulé* is associated with the origins of carnival.

kant [over] v [<Fr *canter*]/to lean, to be slanted]. The term *kant over* means 'to topple over'. E.g., The bucket leanin. Fix it before it *kant over*. [**The bucket is tilted. Fix it before it topples over.**]

kapich n [prob < Fr *capuche*/hood]. Insincere flattery. The term has the sense of pulling the wool over someone's eyes using flattery.

kaptenn bwa n [<Fr *capitaine bois*]/captain wood. A shrub found in Grenada and other Caribbean islands.

karenaj n [<Fr *carénage*]/careenage. Grenada's carenage is a picturesque waterfront located in the heart of the island's capital, St. George's.

kas n [<Fr *casse*]/cassia. A tall tree that produces cylindrical, brownish pods. *Kas* is used in traditional medicine to treat constipation and to get rid of intestinal worms. Scientific name: *Cassia fistula*.

kasé tèt n [<Fr *tête cassée*]/broken head. Term used to refer to nutmeg saplings that sprout under nutmeg trees. These plants are often uprooted, the stems broken off and discarded and the remaining nutmegs retained for use. The term *kasé tèt* therefore refers to the process of breaking off the stem (head) of the nutmeg sapling.

kawé adj [<Fr *carré*]/square. To walk expressively or to strike a pose as if preparing to fight. Some may remember the calypso lyrics 'if you see Monica *kawé*'.

kawèm n [<Fr *carême*]/Lent. Used in some parts of Grenada to refer to the dry season.

ki int pr [<Fr *qui*]/who. The interrogative pronoun *ki* in Kéyòl conveys scepticism. E.g., He say he gettin married next year. *Ki* married! Somebody go married with he? [**He says that he is getting married next year. What nonsense! Who will marry him?**]

kobo n [<Fr *corbeau*]/crow. A large, black bird common in Grenada. [Idiom: Playin dead to catch *kobo* alive. Meaning: Feigning ignorance in order to gather more information or gain the upper hand in a situation.]

kòdon vélon n [<Fr *corde [de] violon*]. From the French term meaning 'violin string', the term *kòdon vélon* refers to a fern-like plant used in traditional medicine to treat colds and stomach aches. Scientific name: *Lygodium venustum*.

kòki [eye] adj [<Fr *coq-l'oeuil*]/cross-eyed.

kokiyé [broom] n [<Fr *cocotier*]/coconut tree. A stiff broom, often used to sweep yards, made from the branches of the coconut tree.

komès n [<Fr *commerce*]/business. Conflict or strife associated with tale bearing or gossiping. E.g., All you stop talkin about the woman husband. I don't have time for all this *komès*. [**Stop discussing the woman's husband. I don't have time for all this strife.**]

kompè n [<Fr *compère*]/comrade, friend. Used to refer to or greet a male friend. E.g., Ay ay, *kompè*, long time no see! [**My goodness, my friend. Long time no see!**]

Kompè Tig n [<Fr *compère*]/comrade, friend + [*tigre*]/tiger. A character in Grenadian Anansi storytelling that is derived from African folklore. See Storytelling and Folklore above.

Kompè Zayen n [<Fr *compère*/comrade, friend + [<Fr *les araignées*]/spiders. In Anansi storytelling, the character Anansi is a quick-witted trickster who takes the form of a spider. In Grenadian folklore and storytelling, Kompè Zayen is equivalent to Anansi. See Storytelling and Folklore above.

komplo n [<Fr *complot*]/plot.

kondisyon n [<Fr *cornichon*]/gherkin. Refers to a tree that bears a highly acidic, light green, elongated fruit. In Grenada, the *kondisyon* fruit is currently used as a pickle and was once used to bleach clothing. Scientific name: *Averrhoa bilimbi*.

Illustration 5.8 The *kondisyon* fruit (*Averrhoa bilimbi*)
This small, bright green, highly acidic fruit
was once used to bleach or remove stains from clothing.

kònn vb [<Fr *corne*]/horn. To be unfaithful. While 'horn' is used widely in Grenada, *kònn* is still heard in some parts of the island. E.g., My wife think I *kònnin* her, but is not true. [**My wife thinks I'm being unfaithful to her, but that is not true.**]

konnsomé vb [<Fr *consommer*]/to consume or use up [food]. Used in the context of allowing food, particularly meats, to absorb seasoning or marinate. E.g., I season me chicken and put it in the fridge to *konnsomé*. [**I seasoned my chicken and put it in the fridge to marinate.**]

kosol matlo n [<Fr *corossol matelot*]/sailor's soursop. This tree is very similar to the common soursop tree in Grenada, the main difference being that the *kosol matlo* fruit becomes yellow when ripe (as opposed to remaining green in the case of the more common soursop fruit).

kòsto adj [<Fr *costaud*]/beefy, robust [person].

koté-si-koté-la exp [<Fr *côté-ci, côté-là*]/this side, that side. Term used to refer to idle and long-winded chatter. E.g., She tell us how

the neighbour husband beatin her, how every night is noise in the house, how the wife fed up, *koté-si-koté-là*. [**She told us that the neighbour's husband is beating her, that there is commotion in the house every night, that the wife is fed up of the situation, and this and that.**]

kotjinil   n [<Fr *cochenille*]/cochineal. A cactus-like plant that bears a reddish flower. The pulp of the plant is sometimes used as a natural shampoo in Grenada. Also known as *rakèt*. Scientific name: *Opuntia cochenillifera.*

kou   adj [prob <Fr *croupir*]/to stagnate, to grow foul. Smelly, having a foul odour.

koubaril   n [<Fr *courbaril*]. The wood of this tree is used as timber. The tree produces a hard, brown pod with an edible pulp inside. Because of the odour of this pulp, the fruit is also known as 'stinking toe'. Scientific name: *Hymenaea courbaril.*

koubé   adj [<Fr *courbé*]/bent. Used to describe someone in a bent or curled-up posture.

koukou pwè   n [cou-cou + <Fr *pois*]/peas. Cou-cou, a popular dish in a number of Caribbean islands, is a cornmeal mixture eaten with fish and meats. The word 'cou-cou' is derived from several West African languages (e.g., Twi, *kúku*) (Winer 2009, 243) and is used to refer to a corn-based dish. *Koukou pwè* is the Carriacouan variety of this similar dish, with peas added to the cornmeal mixture.

koupé   n [<Fr *coupé*]/cut. Term used in the context of kite flying. Refers to the act of cutting the string used to fly a kite to make it blow away.

koupyon   n [<Fr *croupion*]/coccyx or tailbone. Used in reference to chickens. E.g., I love stew chicken; the *koupyon* is my favourite part. [**I love stewed chicken. My favourite part is the tail bone.**]

kouzenn maho   n [<Fr *cousin*] + [*maho*]. A fairly common shrub in Grenada. The term *kouzenn* is derived from the French term for 'cousin' (in the sense of being related or similar to); *maho* is a Kalinago word referring to any category of plants or trees whose barks could be used to make rope. Scientific name: *Urena lobata.*

krapo n [<Fr *crapaud*]/toad. [Idiom: *Krapo* smoke you pipe. Meaning: You will be in a bind or difficult situation.] [Proverb: What is joke for school children is death for *krapo*. Meaning: A situation that seems amusing to one person may be tragic to another.]

krapo (belly) n [<Fr *crapaud*]/toad. Poor or illegible handwriting.

kristofin n [<Fr *cristophine*]/christophene. A light green fruit eaten as a vegetable in Grenada. Known as *cho-cho* in Jamaica. Scientific name: *Sechium edule*.

kutlis n [<Fr *coutelas*]/machete or cutlass.

kwadril n [<Fr *quadrille*]/quadrille. A dance once popular in Grenada and still popular in Carriacou. See Folk Songs, Carnival and Calypso above.

kwè kay n [<Fr *coin [de la] case*]/corner [of the] hut. A plant that grows close to the corner of houses in Grenada and is used in traditional medicine for kidney ailments.

labas n [<Fr *la basse*]/sandbank, shoal. An open-air dump.

ladjablès n [<Fr *la diablesse*]/she-devil. A figure in Grenadian folklore. See Storytelling and Folklore above.

lahé v [prob <Fr *lâcher*]/to loosen or slacken. To idle or fail to apply oneself to a task or job. E.g., Give me the broom let me sweep the house; I don't have time to *lahé*. [**Give me the broom to sweep the house. I don't have time to waste.**]

lajinè n [<Fr *l'angelin*]/cabbage tree. A tall tree whose wood is used in the construction of wooden homes. The bark of this tree is also considered to have anthelmintic properties. Scientific name: *Andira inermis*.

lakampayn n [<Fr *la campagne*]/the countryside. Term used in Grenada to refer to a wake, more common in the rural parts of the island, which is held to pray and sing songs in remembrance of a deceased person. These wakes are now more commonly known in Grenada as 'three nights prayers', as they are held three nights after the death of an

individual. 'Three nights prayers' are generally followed by 'nine nights prayers'. (See video **Chapter 2: Religious and Spiritual Expression**; *Lakampayn (Prayer for the Deceased): Discussion and Songs* video clip.)

lakwas n [<Fr *la crasse*]/filth, scum. Dirt or scum from one's body.

lali n [prob <Fr *la lie*]/dregs. Moss or slime on stones.

lambi n [<Fr *lambi*]/stromb or conch. A mollusc or shell of the genus *Strombus*. *Lambi* is eaten in a wide variety of dishes in Grenada and several other Caribbean islands. The term *lambi* is likely derived from *lambic*, the elided form of the French word *alambic* (English: a distillation apparatus used with a siphon, a still.) The manuscript *Histoire de L'Isle de Grenade en Amérique: 1649-1659* (see page 12) describes the dire situation faced by Grenada's residents resulting from conflict on the island during the 1649-1659 period as follows: *'la faim les contrainct à manger des crables, des burgots, des lambics rien que vilainies et qu'ordures'*[9] (Roget, comp. (1659) 1975, 113) ['hunger forced them to eat crabs, whelks, and lambis—anything but waste or garbage']. For the indigenous people of the Caribbean, including those of Grenada, the *lambi* had a variety of nutritional, ornamental and functional uses that were passed on to the enslaved. The *lambi* shell was once blown by runaway slaves to communicate with each other and continues to retain special significance in Grenada and other Caribbean islands (see *nèg mawon*). In Grenada, it is still used as a means of communication—to inform communities that a vehicle selling fish is passing by and at carnival time, particularly on *jouvé* morning, when the blowing of the *lambi* shell usually signals the start of carnival festivities on that day.

latjé chat n [< Fr *la queue [du] chat*]/cat's tail. This plant bears a long, red, tail-like flower. Scientific name: *Acalypha hispida*.

---

[9] Middle French (fourteenth to early seventeenth centuries)—the intermediate linguistic period preceding modern French.

Illustration 5.9 *Lambi* (conch) shells
Used as ornaments in a yard in Grenada.

Illustration 5.10 The *latjé chat* plant (*Acalypha hispida*)
Also known as cat's tail.

lavwé n [<Fr *la voix*]/voice. *Lavwé* refers to singing in a loud voice, especially in a Carnival context.

lawa fré fré adj [prob <Fr *la roi*]/king + [*se frayer*]/to fight one's way. Used in the context of stick fighting (*kalinda*) in Grenada. Stick fighters fought for the title of king. *Kalinda* is one of the precursors of carnival. Perhaps because the term (in its entirety) is associated with stick fighting, the word *lawa* in Grenadian Kéyòl refers to a loud, coarse and overly aggressive woman.

ligarou n [<Fr *loupgarou*]/werewolf. See Storytelling and Folklore above.

lòriyé n [<Fr *laurier*]/laurel tree. Tall rainforest tree. Scientific name: *Ocotea martinicensis*.

mach imp vb [<Fr *marcher*]/walk. The term *mach* is used to chase dogs away. E.g., *Mach* dog! [**Go away, dog!**]

machann n [<Fr *marchand*]/a market or street vendor.

maché a tè n [<Fr *marcher à terre*]/walk on the ground. A vine used in traditional medicine for kidney ailments.

makafouchèt n [<Fr *manquer la fourchette*]/miss the fork. Leftover food—from the image of food that has 'missed the fork' and remained on one's plate.

makak n [<Fr *macaque*]/monkey. The French word *macaque* is a loan word from the Bantu language group, in which '*ma*' serves as a plural marker and '*kaku*' means 'monkey'.

makmè n [<Fr *ma commère*]. This term, which literally means 'my co-mother', refers to a godmother. The term is generally used to refer to or greet a good friend or to refer to someone with whom one has a close personal relationship.

makmè fam n [<Fr *ma commère*]/see *makmè* above + [<Fr *femme*]/ woman. A *makmè fam* refers to a man who behaves in a fussy or effeminate way.

mako n [<Fr *ma commère*]/see *makmè* above. *Mako* is a shortened version of the Kéyòl term *makmè* (see definition above) and refers to someone who is overly inquisitive and prone to prying and snooping. The adjective *makocious* (also spelled *macocious*) (nosey) has been coined from the word *mako*.

mal èstomak n [<Fr *mal estomac*]/bad stomach. A shrub used in traditional medicine for pain and fever. Scientific name: *Piper amalago*.

maldjo n [<Fr *mal* + *yeux*]/bad eye. According to Grenadian mythology, *maldjo* is an illness contracted by a young child when someone with evil intent looks at him or her (with an evil eye).

malkadi n [<Fr *mal caduc*]/epilepsy. The French term *mal caduc* is archaic; the Kéyòl term *malkadi* is still used in Grenada to refer to epilepsy.

mal lévé adj [<Fr *mal lévé*]/ill-bred, badly brought up. Used to describe ill-mannered or insolent children.

mal pouwi n [<Fr *mal*]/bad + [<Fr *pourri*]/rotten. This plant is also known in Grenada as *kojo root*, in Jamaica as *Guinea hen weed* and in other islands as *mawi pouwi*. The leaves of this plant have a pungent odour. In traditional medicine, it is used to treat arthritis and allergies and is also believed to kill cancer cells. Scientific name: *Petiveria alliacea*.

mama glo n [<Fr *maman de l'eau*]/mother of the water. Term derived from the Yoruba religion. Often used in a secular sense to refer to a mermaid. In a religious (Yoruba) context, *mama glo* refers to the *orisha* (deity) Yemanja, the spirit of the water. See Storytelling and Folklore above.

mama maladi n [<Fr *maman*] mother (informal) + [<Fr *maladie*]/ sickness. See Storytelling and Folklore above.

mamapoul n [<Fr *maman poule*]/mother hen. Someone who fusses unnecessarily.

mamzèl n [<Fr *mademoiselle*]/miss. Term of familiarity used to address or greet a woman.

[mango] bèf n [<Fr *boeuf*]/beef. A type of fleshy mango in Grenada.

manjé kochon n [<Fr *manger*]/eat, feed + [<Fr *cochon*]/pig. A vine that grows wild in Grenada. Used by children as a skipping rope.

manjé pòpòt n [<Fr *manger*]/eat, feed + [<Fr *poupée*]/doll. The term is derived from the notion of children playing with dolls' houses and refers to childish or silly games. E.g., All you don't see how those politicians behavin? Real *manjé pòpòt, wi*. [**Don't you see the behaviour of those politicians? It really is childish and silly.**]

maotjè n [prob <Fr *(avoir) mal au coeur*]/to feel queasy. A type of seaweed that washes ashore in Grenada and is used as a fertiliser. This seaweed is different from the kind used to make the Grenadian seaweed drink known as 'seamoss'.

marenn n [<Fr *marraine*]/godmother.

matité n [<Fr *maturité*]/maturity. Term used to describe a child who acts older than his/her age.

melondjen n [<Fr *mélongène*]/eggplant, aubergine.

mèm bagay n [<Fr *même bagage*]/same baggage. In French-lexicon Creole, *bagay* means 'thing'. *Mèm bagay* therefore means 'same thing'.

milit n [<Fr *mulette*]/freshwater or river mussel. In Grenada, a small, greyish black, freshwater fish.

modan n [<Fr *mordant*]/biting. The claws of a crab.

modi adj [<Fr *maudit*]/accursed. E.g., That boy Alex *modi* and wayward too much. [**Alex is a very troublesome and wayward boy.**]

mortèl n [<Fr *immortel*]/immortal. A prickly tree common in Grenada that bears red flowers. Often used as a shade tree. Scientific name: *Erythrina poeppigiana*.

mouch è fè n [<Fr *mouche à feu*]/firefly.

mové lang vb [<Fr *mauvaise langue*]/bad tongue. Destructive and malicious gossip. E.g., I fraid Mary. She like to *mové lang* people too much. [**I'm afraid of Mary. She gossips too much.**]

mwen ka alé exp [<Fr *moi*]/me + [<Fr *aller*]/to go. The Kéyòl expression, which translates as 'I am going', is often used by Kéyòl speakers and aficionados to signal familiarity with or fondness for the Kéyòl language. *Ka* is a tense marker in the Kéyòl language.

mwen wivé exp [<Fr *moi*]/me + [<Fr *arriver*]/arrive. The Grenadian English-lexicon Creole equivalent of this Kéyòl expression is 'I reach'. Standard English equivalent: I'm here.

[my] hont n [<Fr *honte*]/shame. A plant given this name because the leaves fold inward when touched. Also known in Grenada as 'shame bush', 'sensitive plant', 'six o'clock bush' and 'scorn the earth'. Scientific name: *Mimosa pudica*.

Illustration 5.11 The *my hont* plant (*Mimosa pudica*)
Also known as shame bush.

nèg mawon n [<Fr *nègre marron*]/runaway slave. In many Caribbean islands, including Grenada, slaves escaped the horrors of slavery by running away and hiding in dense forests, subsisting on hunting and, in some cases, farming. They sometimes formed alliances with the indigenous people in an effort to evade their European captors. Sizeable maroon communities were formed in a number of islands, including Dominica, St. Vincent and Jamaica. Both Dominica and Haiti have statues in their capitals honouring the *nèg mawon*. In both instances, the *nèg mawon* is depicted blowing a conch (*lambi*) shell.

nòm bon nòm n [<Fr *homme bon homme*]. This herb, also known as 'man-better-man', is used in traditional medicine to treat a variety of ailments, among them flu-like symptoms. It is also prepared as an infusion to treat diabetes. Scientific name: *Achyranthes aspera.*

nom fosé adj [<Fr *homme* + *forcé*]. Term used to describe a child (*homme*/man) who appears to have matured too quickly (*forcé*/forced). In Grenadian English-lexicon Creole, the term used is 'force ripe' and is also used to refer to fruits that fail to ripen properly because they were harvested before becoming fully mature.

non n [<Fr *non*]/no. Used as a tag or marker in Grenadian English-lexicon Creole for the purpose of emphasis. E.g., Stop fightin *non*! [**Please stop fighting!**]

pa/ba konnè phr [<Fr *pas*]/not + [<Fr *connaître*]/know. The Kéyòl phrase means 'I don't know'.

pap n [<Fr *pâte*]/paste. A kind of porridge made by adding a small amount of water to flour over a fire and turning it into a paste. The porridge is called *flour pap*.

papa-yo excl [<Fr *papa*]/father (informal). Exclamatory expression used to convey surprise or admiration. E.g., She come first in exams again. *Papa-yo*, this child bright *wi*! [**She came first in her examinations again. Wow! This child is really intelligent!**]

parenn n [<Fr *parrain*]/godfather.

paté n [<Fr *pâté*]/pie. A small turnover (or *empanada*) filled with meat, usually beef. Generally served as a hors d'oeuvre in Grenada.

Paywo n [<Fr *Pierrot*]. A carnival masquerader who was once popular in Grenada and Carriacou. The term is derived from Italian *Commedia dell'arte* performances, popular in late seventeenth-century France. The Grenada *short-knee* masquerader, the Carriacou *Shakespeare mas* and the Trinidad *Pierrot Grenade* (Grenada Pierrot) are all linked to the *Paywo* masquerader. See Folksongs, Carnival and Calypso above.

pènépis n [<Fr *pain d'épice*]/gingerbread. A tree that bears an orange-coloured edible fruit. This fruit is a favourite of the Mona monkey that largely inhabits the Grand Étang forest in Grenada (Hawthorne 2004, 22). Scientific name: *Pouteria multiflora.*

pépsi adj [prob <Fr *pépie*]/pip (a bird ailment marked by a scaly tongue) or parched. The Kéyòl term *pépsi* means 'unattractive' or 'bland'.

pika n [<Fr *piquant*]/thorn, prickle.

pisennli n [<Fr *pissenlit*]/bed-wetter.

piti bom n [<Fr *petit baume*]. The French term translates literally as 'small balsam'. *Piti bom* is similar to the basil plant and is used in traditional medicine in Grenada to treat colds and flu-like symptoms. Scientific name: *Ocimum campechianum.*

Illustration 5.12 The *piti bom* plant (*Ocimum campechianum*)
This plant is used to treat the common cold.

piti fè adv [<Fr *petites affaires*]. From the French term meaning 'small business', the term *piti fè* refers to business done, transacted or arranged in secret.

piti jou n [<Fr *petit jour*]/daybreak.

planas n [<Fr *plan* + *asséner*]. The French term *plan* means 'flat' and the word *asséner* means 'to strike', so this word means a blow given with the flat part of a cutlass (machete). E.g., If you keep on makin noise, I givin you one *planas*; that go keep you quiet. [**If you don't stop your noise, you'll get a spanking. That will force you to be quiet.**]

plantè n [<Fr *plantain*]/plantain. Small shrub used in traditional medicine to treat earaches and as a poultice to treat eye disorders. Scientific name: *Plantago major*.

po n [<Fr *pot [de chambre]*]/chamber pot, potty.

podjab n [<Fr *pauvre diable*]/poor devil. Someone who appears to be pitiful or lonely. E.g., Girl how you stand up there lookin like a *podjab* so? [**Girl why are you standing there looking so pitiful?**]

pòm kanèl n [<Fr *pomme cannelle*]/sugar apple. The Kéyòl term *pòm kanèl* is used to express endearment or affection in Grenada.

pòm woz n [<Fr *pomme rose*]/rose apple. A light yellow, round, rose-scented fruit. Scientific name: *Syzygium jambos.* Also a place name in Grenada.

ponch a krèm n [<Fr *ponche à crème*]/cream punch. A Christmas beverage made of rum, eggs and milk or cream.

popo n [<Fr *poupée*]/doll. The Kéyòl term *popo* means 'baby'.

poto légiz n [<Fr *poste de l'église*]/church post. Someone who goes to church so frequently or is so active in the church that he or she is considered a post or pillar of the church.

pou poul n [<Fr *poux poule*]/fowl lice.

pouyen n [<Fr *pour rien*]/for nothing, free of charge.

pwa dou n [<Fr *pois doux*]/sweet peas. A tall evergreen that bears a pod containing an edible white fruit whose flavour is similar to the vanilla bean. Scientific name: *Inga edulis*.

pwa gaté n [<Fr *pois*]/peas + [<Fr *gratté*]/itching, scratching. A vine in Grenada that bears dark brown pods. The hairs found on these pods cause severe itching. Also known as 'cow itch'. Scientific name: *Mucuna pruriens*.

pwangad excl [<Fr *prends garde*]/be careful! Watch out!

pwèl n [<Fr *poil*]/[body] hair. Pubic hair.

pyan n [<Fr *pian*]/yaws. Any kind of sore.

raf n [<Fr *rafle*]/raid. This term is largely associated with the playing of marbles—grabbing or raiding the marbles of other children.

rak adj [prob <Fr *âpre*]/sour. The Kéyòl term *rak* means 'brackish' or 'slightly sour'.

rakèt n [<Fr *raquette*]/prickly pear. Synonym for *kotjinil*.

rèkonnèt v [<Fr *reconnaître*]/recognise. Used in the sense of going to see what is happening. E.g., I hear a noise down the road. I goin and *rèkonnèt*. [**I heard a noise in the road. I'm going to see what is happening.**]

sa pr [<Fr *ça*]/that. *Sa* is used to convey dismissiveness or contempt. E.g., He say he goin in America next month. *Ki* America *sa*? He never even been in St. George's. [**He says he's going to America next month. What America is that? He's never even been to St. George's.**]

sabo n [<Fr *sabot*]/clog. Any kind of old shoe.

sakajé adj [<Fr *saccagé*]/vandalised, wrecked.

sa ki fè ou exp [<Fr *ça + qui + faire*]. Grenadian English-lexicon Creole equivalent: What do you? Standard English equivalent: What's wrong with you?

sa ki tan, palé lòt exp [<Fr *ceux qui entendent, parlez aux autres*]. Literally translated as 'those who hear, tell the others', this Kéyòl expression was once widely used in Grenada to mean 'spread the word'.

sakwé salòp adj vulg [<Fr *sacré salop*]/damn bastard.

salé n [<Fr *salé*]/salty.

salòp n [<Fr *salop*]/bastard. Generally used to refer to children who misbehave.

sapòt n [<Fr *sapote*]/sapota. A tree of the sapodilla family. In Grenada, only the seed of this tree's fruit is used and serves as a spice to flavour baked goods. In other countries such as Cuba, the brownish-orange flesh of the fruit is eaten. Scientific name: *Pouteria sapota*.

sa sé tout sé mèm exp [<Fr *ça + c'est + tout + c'est + même*]. The Kéyòl expression means 'it's all the same; it all comes down to the same thing'.

sésé n [<Fr *soeur*]/sister.

sikiyé [fig] n [<Fr *sucrier*]/sugar, sugar-producing. A finger-sized banana prized for its sweetness. In Grenada and Trinidad, the term *fig* is generally synonymous with any type of banana. Ripe *figs* are eaten as fruits; green *figs* are cooked in a variety of ways.

simen kontwa n [<Fr *semences contre [les vers]*]/seeds to prevent [worms]. The Kéyòl term is originally derived from the Latin term *semen contra*, an abbreviated form of the entire term *semen contra vermes*. *Simen kontwa* refers to a medicinal herb used to treat persons or animals infected with worms and other parasites. Also known as 'vermifuge'. Scientific name: *Chenopodium ambrosioides*.

sòt adj [<Fr *sotte (f)*]/foolish, silly.

soula n [<Fr *soûlard*]/drunk.

soungou n [prob <Fr *sans goût*]/without taste. Term used to describe a person who shows a lack of energy or spirit.

souplé n [<Fr *s'il vous plaît*]/please.

sov ki pou exp [<Fr *sauve qui peut*]/each man for himself.

[sweet man] doré exp [<Fr *doré*]/golden. A man who dresses in a flamboyant way to impress others.

takté adj [<Fr *tacheté*]/spotted, speckled. Persons with marks or spots on their skin. Also used to describe overripe fruits, especially mangoes, with dark spots.

tambou bambou n [<Fr *tambour bambou*]/bamboo drum. Bamboo musical instruments once made by the enslaved. The *tambou bambou* is considered to have played a key role in the development of modern carnival instruments. See Folksongs, Carnival and Calypso above.

tanti n [<Fr *tante*]/aunt.

tatou n [<Fr *tatou*]/armadillo.

tébé n [prob <Fr *débat*]/discussion, inner turmoil. The Grenadian Kéyòl term *tébé* refers to conflict and strife often linked to gossiping.

tèchnè n [<Fr *tête [du] chien*]/dog's head. A long, black, slippery, snake-like fish found in rivers and wet, muddy areas under stones.

terin n [<Fr *terrine*]/earthenware bowl.

tété n [<Fr *tétée*]/breast-feeding. A woman's breasts.

tjè bèf n [<Fr *coeur [du] boeuf*]. Literally cow's heart, the term refers to the custard apple fruit. Scientific name: *Annona reticulata*.

tjè bon n [<Fr *coeur bon*]/good heart. A variety of mango in Grenada.

tjou kako n [<Fr *chou cacao*]/cabbage cocoa. A spinach-like plant eaten in Grenada.

tjou poul excl phr vulg [<Fr *trou du cul*]/asshole. Term used to convey disgust or dismissiveness. E.g., If he want police to arrest him,

tjou poul! I can't bother! [**If he wants the police to arrest him, that's his business. I can't be bothered.**]

tjwé mwa on fwa n [<Fr *tuez moi une fois*]/kill me once. This plant bears a pinkish flower. Scientific name: *Cybianthus antillanus*.

tòchon n [Fr<*torchon*]/rag. The loofah sponge gourd, derived from the *Luffa aegyptiaca* plant.

ton n [<Fr *thon*]/tuna.

tonnè excl phr [<Fr *tonnerre*]/thunder. Used to convey admiration for something said or done. E.g., How you dress up so? *Tonnè*! [**Why are you so dressed up? Wow!**]

touché donk la exp [<Fr *touchez donc là*]/Touch it here. This expression, usually accompanied by an outstretched hand inviting a handshake, is used to commend someone on something well said or well done, particularly during a discussion.

touf-touf n [<Fr *touffe*]/clump, cluster. The reduplicative term refers to someone of short stature and heavy build.

toulémwa n [<Fr *tous les mois*]/every month (Allsopp 2003, 563). The roots of this lily-like plant were once used to obtain arrowroot starch. Scientific name: *Canna edulis*.

tout bagay n [<Fr *tout bagage*]/all the baggage. Very common Kéyòl term, used in many Caribbean islands where French-lexicon Creole is spoken, meaning 'everything', 'the whole lot' or 'the works'.

tout moun n [<Fr *tout [le] monde*]/everyone.

tout moun annsam exp [<Fr *tout [le] monde ensemble*]/everyone together.

toutoulbé adj [<Fr *tituber*]/to stagger or reel. Dismayed or upset to the point of appearing dazed or stunned.

troché vb [<Fr *troquer*]/to barter, to exchange.

[twa] malewèz exp [<Fr *malhereux*]/wretched or unfortunate person. The expression *twa malewèz* is used to curse someone. The

expression is usually accompanied by spitting (hence the use of the onomatopoeic word *twa* to capture the sound of spitting). E.g., *Twa malewèz*! You little tief!! [**You wretched little thief!**]

twavo n [<Fr *travaux*]/work. Someone who does road repair work.

twèf n [<Fr *trèfle*]/trefoil, clover, climbing plant with three leaflets. Used to treat intestinal worms. Scientific name: *Aristolochia trilobata*.

vaps n [prob <Fr *vapes*]/to be in the clouds, to be out of it. The term refers to actions taken impulsively or with little or no forethought. E.g., He catch a *vaps* and decide he goin and cut down the tree. [**Something got into his head and he decided to cut down the tree.**]

vaykivay adv [<Fr *vaille que vaille*]/somehow or the other, come what may. *Vaykivay* describes the attitude of someone who does things in an impromptu, unplanned way; someone who seems to have no cares or worries.

venn-venn n [<Fr *verveine*]/vervain. A bitter herb that produces purple or white flowers. The leaves of this herb are boiled and drunk to treat a variety of ailments. Scientific name: *Stachytarpheta jamaicensis*.

vètivè n [<Fr *vétiver (archaic)*]/vertiver. A tall, grassy plant. The sweet-smelling root of the *vètivè* plant is used as a fragrance to keep stored clothing smelling fresh. Scientific name: *Vetiveria zizanioides*.

vini v [<Fr *venir*]/to come.

vini tout moun exp [<Fr *venir + tout le monde*]/come, everyone.

vyéko n [<Fr *vieux corps*]/old body. A carnival character whose dress was originally old black clothing and clogs. The *vyékos* come from the Victoria and Gouyave areas of Grenada. While the Victoria *vyékos* wear dark-coloured costumes, the costumes of the Gouyave *vyékos* are more colourful. See section on Folksongs, Carnival and Calypso above.

In Dominican French-lexicon Creole, the term *vyékò* is used to mean 'old man'.

vyé nèg n [<Fr *vieux nègre*]/old nigger. A pejorative, racist term used to describe someone perceived to belong to the lower echelons of society.

wajé n [<Fr *hallier*]/thicket, dense shrubbery. Many herbs, grasses and plants in Grenada (and in other French-lexicon-Creole-speaking Caribbean islands), particularly those used in traditional medicine, begin with *wajé* (*razié* in Martinique) or *zèb* (see definition of *zèb*).

wajé pété n vulg [<Fr *hallier*]/thicket + [*pété*]/fart. Synonym for *dégoflé* (see definition). Scientific name: *Hyptis capitata*.

wamajé vb [<Fr *ramager*]/to sing, to chirp. Ad lib singing, generally of calypsos.

wentè adj [prob <Fr *pointer*]/to jut out, to protrude. Someone of thin stature or build.

wi n [<Fr *oui*]/yes. Used as a tag or marker in Grenadian English-lexicon Creole for the purpose of emphasis. E.g., Lord, outside hot *wi*! [**Lord, it really is hot outdoors!**]

wi fout excl phr [<Fr *oui, foutre*]/Yes, damn it! An expression used to convey surprise and, in some instances, admiration. E.g., *Wi fout*! Girl how you dress up so? [**Damn it, girl, why are you so dressed up?**]

wi papa excl phr [<Fr *oui papa*]/Yes father! An expression generally used to convey admiration.

yann gaté n [<Fr *liane grattée*]/scratching vine. This vine is used by children as a skipping rope.

zaboka n [<Fr *les avocats*]/avocados. Scientific name: *Persea Americana*.

zafè exp [<Fr *les affaires*]/business. The word *zafè* in the possessive form is equivalent to saying 'that's your business'. E.g., So you don't want to go in the shop for me? *Zafè* you! [**So you don't want to go to the shop for me? That's your business!**]

zagada n [<Fr *lézard regardant*]/looking lizard. A type of lizard common in Grenada.

zami n [<Fr *les amis*]/friends. A lesbian relationship.

zangi n [<Fr *les anguilles*] (Allsopp 2003, 623)/eel. A freshwater eel caught in rivers and eaten in Grenada.

zèb n [<Fr *les herbes*]/grass. Many herbs, grasses and plants in Grenada (and other French-lexicon-Creole-speaking Caribbean islands), particularly those used in traditional medicine, begin with *zèb* or *wajé* (see definition of *wajé*).

zèbafam n [<Fr *les herbes à femme*]/women's herb. A short herb used widely in traditional medicine to treat a variety of ailments including pains associated with menstrual cramps, hence its name. Scientific name: *Ageratum conyzoides*.

zèbakonèt n [prob <Fr *les herbes + à + connaître*]/knowledge grass. Used in traditional medicine to treat a wide variety of ailments.

zèbapik n [<Fr *les herbes + à + pique*]/pricking grass. A bitter herb widely used in traditional medicine to treat a variety of ailments, particularly colds and fever. Scientific name: *Neurolaena lobata*.

Illustration 5.13 The *zèbapik* plant (*Neurolaena lobata*)
This plant is used to treat colds and infections.

zèb anmè n [<Fr *les herbes amères*]/bitter grass. A bitter herb used in traditional medicine for fever and constipation.

zèb chyen n [<Fr *les herbes + chien*]/dog grass. Fine grass with a distinctive odour.

zèb glo n [<Fr *les herbes + eau*]/water grass. A grass often used to feed pigs.

zèb kalbach n [<Fr *les herbes + calebasse*]/calabash grass. A vine-like plant that produces a gourd or fruit very similar to the calabash tree, but smaller.

zèb kouto n [<Fr *les herbes + couteau*]/knife grass. Also known as 'razor grass'. Scientific name: *Scleria scindens*.

zèb savan n [<Fr *les herbes + savane*]/pasture grass. Also known as 'savannah grass' and 'carpet grass'. Scientific name: *Axonopus compressus*.

zèb sépantjé n [<Fr *les herbes + charpentier*]/carpenter grass. A pleasant-smelling grass used in traditional medicine as a relaxant and, perhaps because of its anti-inflammatory properties, also to dress wounds. Scientific name: *Justicia pectoralis*.

zèb zédri n [<Fr *les herbes + aiguilles*]/needle grass. In traditional medicine, the leaves of this plant are used to treat kidney ailments. Scientific name: *Bidens pilosa*.

Illustration 5.14 The *zèb zédri* plant (*Bidens pilosa*)
Also known as needle grass.

zéglèt n [<Fr *les aiglettes*]/egrets, herons. Term used to describe someone of thin or slight build.

zépina n [<Fr *les épinards*]/spinach. This edible plant is known as *callaloo* in Jamaica but as *zépina* in Grenada. In Grenada, *callaloo* is made from taro or dasheen leaves. *Zépina* is also known in some countries as 'vegetable amaranth'. Scientific name: *Amaranthus viridis.*

zong chat n [<Fr *les ongles [du] chat*]/cat's claws. A vine that grows on trees and clings tightly to tree barks. Scientific name: *Macfadyena unguis-cati.*

zounks n [prob <Fr *les onces*]/ounces. Term used to refer to a very small amount of food or drink left over after cooking.

zouti n [<Fr *les orties*]/nettle. Scientific name: *Dalechampia scandens.*

zowey kabwit n [<Fr *les oreilles [du] cabri*]/goat's ears. A variety of spinach eaten in Grenada. Often grows under cocoa trees.

6

REFERENCES

Allsopp, Richard, ed. 2013. *Dictionary of Caribbean English Usage*. Kingston: University of the West Indies Press.

Beckles, Hilary McDonald. 2008. "Kalinago (Carib) Resistance to European Colonisation of the Caribbean". *Caribbean Quarterly* 54 (4): 77-94.

Boomert, Arie. 2003. "Agricultural Societies in the Continental Caribbean". In *General History of the Caribbean, Vol 1, Autochthonous Societies*. Edited by Jalil Sued-Badillo. 6 vols. Paris: UNESCO Publishing.

Brinkley, Frances Kay. 1978. "An Analysis of the 1750 Carriacou Census". *Caribbean Quarterly* 24 (1-2): 44-60.

Brizan, George. 1984. *Grenada – Island of Conflict: From Amerindians to People's Revolution, 1498-1979*. London: Zed Books.

Dalphinis, Morgan. 1985. *Caribbean and African Languages: Social History, Language, Literature and Education*. London: Karia Press.

DeCamp, David. 1968. "The Field of Creole Language Studies". *Latin American Research Review* 3 (3): 25-46.

Devas, Raymund P. 1932. *Conception Island, or the Troubled Story of the Catholic Church in Grenada, B.W.I.* London: Sands and Co.

———. 1974. *The History of the Island of Grenada, 1498-1796*. St. George's, Grenada: Carenage Press.

Diagana, Ousmane Moussa. 2013. *Dictionnaire Soninké-Français (Mauritanie)* [Soninke-French Dictionary (Mauritania)]. Paris: Karthala.

Du Tertre, Jean-Baptiste. 1667. *Histoire Générale des Antilles Habitées par les François.* Vol. 1. Paris: Thomas Jolly.

Hawthorne, William D., Dean Jules, Guido Marcelle and Rosemary Wise. 2004. *Caribbean Spice Island Plants: Trees, Shrubs, and Climbers of Grenada, Carriacou, and Petit Martinique—a Picture Gallery with Notes on Identification, Historical, and Other Trivia.* Oxford: Oxford Forestry Institute.

Hidalgo, Dennis R. 2012. "Africa in the Caribbean: An Overview". *Inform Africa*, June 18. http://www.informafrica.com/african-studies/africa-in-the-caribbean-by-dennis-r-hidalgo/

Holm, John. 1989. *Pidgins and Creoles,* Vol. 2: *Reference Survey.* Cambridge Language Surveys. Cambridge: Cambridge University Press.

Jourdain, Elodie. 1956. *Du Français aux Parlers Créoles.* Paris: Librairie C. Klincksieck.

Laman, K. E. (1936). 1964. Dictionnaire kikongo-français avec une étude phonétique décrivant les dialectes les plus importants de la langue dite kikongo. 2 vols. New Jersey: Gregg Press Inc.

Melzer, Sara E. 2012. *Colonizer or Colonized: The Hidden Stories of Early Modern French Culture.* Philadelphia: University of Pennsylvania Press.

Pardue, Jeff. 1997. "Fédon's Rebellion". In *The Historical Encyclopedia of World Slavery*, Edited by Junius P. Rodriguez. 2 vols. Santa Barbara, CA: ABC-CLIO.

Robert, Paul. 1993. *Le Nouveau Petit Robert: Dictionnaire de la Langue Française.* Paris: Dictionnaires Le Robert.

Roberts, Peter A. 1971. "The Verb in Grenadian French Creole". Master's thesis, University of the West Indies, Jamaica.

———. 1997. *From Oral to Literate Culture: Colonial Experience in the English West Indies.* Kingston: The University Press of the West Indies.

Roget, Jacques Petitjean, comp. (1659) 1975. *Histoire de L'Isle de Grenade en Amérique: 1649-1659*. Montreal: Montreal University Press. Originally published anonymously.

———.1983. *Personnes et Familles à la Martinique au XVIIème Siècle d'après Recensements et Terriers Administratifs*. Fort-de-France: Société d'Histoire de la Martinique.

da Silva Maia, A. 1964. Dicionário complementar português-kimbundu-kikongo. Cucujães: A. Maia da Silva.

Spitzer, Leo. 1966. "Creole Attitudes Towards Krio: An Historical Survey". *Sierra Leone Language Review* 5: 39-43.

Steele, Beverley A. 2003. *Grenada: A History of its People*. Oxford: Macmillan Caribbean.

Taylor, Douglas. 1977. *Languages of the West Indies*. Baltimore: The Johns Hopkins University Press.

Thomas, John Jacob. (1869) 1969. *The Theory and Practice of Creole Grammar*. London: New Beacon Books.

Williams, Eric. 1938. "The Economic Aspect of the Abolition of the West Indian Slave Trade and Slavery". Ph.D. diss., Oxford University.

———. 1970. *From Columbus to Castro: The History of the Caribbean, 1492-1969*. London: Andre Deutsch.

Winer, Lise, ed. 2009. *Dictionary of the English/Creole of Trinidad & Tobago: On Historical Principles*. Montreal: McGill-Queen's University Press.

7

FURTHER READING

Aub-Buscher, Gertrud. 1969. Introduction to *The Theory and Practice of Creole Grammar* by John Jacob Thomas. London: New Beacon Books Ltd.

Carrington, Lawrence D. 1988. *Creole Discourse and Social Development*. Ottawa: International Development Resource Centre.

Cassidy, Frederic Gomes, and Robert B. LePage, eds. 2002. *Dictionary of Jamaican English*. 2nd ed. Kingston: University of the West Indies Press.

Chaudenson, Robert. 2001. *Creolization of Language and Culture*. London: Routledge.

Cowley, John. 1996. *Carnival, Canboulay and Calypso*. Cambridge: Cambridge University Press.

Cox, Edward L. 1984. *Free Coloreds in the Slave Societies of St. Kitts and Grenada, 1763-1833*. Knoxville: University of Tennessee Press.

Crask, Paul. 2009. *Grenada, Carriacou, Petite Martinique: The Bradt Travel Guide*. Chalfont St Peter, England: Bradt Travel Guides.

DeGraff, Michel. 2005. "Linguists' Most Dangerous Myth: The Fallacy of Exceptionalism". *Language in Society* 34: 533-591.

Dictionary of Grenadianisms. Big Drum Nation. http://www.bigdrumnation.org/dictionary.htm

Fontaine, Marcel and Peter A. Roberts. 1991. *Dominica's English-Creole Dictionary*. Roseau, Dominica: The Folk Research Institute.

Frank, David, ed. 2001. *Kwéyòl Dictionary*. Castries, St. Lucia: Ministry of Education.

Hay, John. 1823. *A Narrative of the Insurrection in the Island of Grenada: Which Took Place in 1795*. London: J. Ridgway.

Honychurch, Lennox. "Aspects of Carib/Kalinago Culture". *Lennox Honychurch*. Last modified 2015. http://www.lennoxhonychurch.com/article.cfm?id=389

Martin, John Angus. 2013. *Island Caribs and French Settlers in Grenada*. St. George's: Grenada National Museum Press.

McDaniel, Lorna. 1998. *The Big Drum Ritual of Carriacou: Praisesongs in Memory of Flight*. Gainesville: University Press of Florida.

Mitchell, Edward S. 2010. *St. Lucian Kwéyòl on St. Croix: A Study of Language Choice and Attitudes*. Cambridge: Cambridge Scholars Publishing.

Roberts, Peter A. 1998. *West Indians and Their Language*. Cambridge: Cambridge University Press.

———. 2008. *The Roots of Caribbean Identity*. Cambridge: Cambridge University Press.

Simmons-McDonald, Hazel and Ian Robertson, eds. 2006. *Exploring the Boundaries of Caribbean Creole Languages*. Kingston: University of the West Indies Press.

Smith, Faith. *Creole Recitations: John Jacob Thomas and Colonial Formation in the Late Nineteenth-Century Caribbean*. New World Studies. Charlottesville: University of Virginia Press.

Smith, Michael Garfield, Lambros Comitas, Jack Harewood, and Josep Llobera. 2008. *Education and Society in the Creole Caribbean*. New York: CIFAS.

Valdman, Albert. 2000. "Creole, the Language of Slavery". In *Slavery in the Caribbean Francophone World: Distant Voices, Forgotten Acts, Forged Identities*, edited by Doris Y. Kadish, 143-63. Athens: University of Georgia Press.

Marise La Grenade-Lashley was born in St. George's, Grenada in 1959. After obtaining her secondary education from St. Joseph's Convent and the Grenada Boys' Secondary School, Marise continued her studies in Canada and was awarded a Bachelor's degree in French and Spanish from Mount Saint Vincent University in 1982. In 1984, she earned a Master's degree in Economics from Howard University in Washington, DC and in 1986, a second Master's degree in Translation from the *École de traduction et d' interprétation* (ETI), *Université de Genève* in Switzerland.

Marise's passion for words and language led her to devote more than 25 years of her life to the translating profession in Washington, DC, working from French, Spanish and Portuguese to English. She started her career at the United States Department of State as a staff translator and later joined the World Bank, where she headed the English Translation Team for over 10 years.

Over the years, Marise has maintained strong ties with her native Grenada, where she now spends most of her time.

MULTIMEDIA CONTENT

To access the enhanced multimedia content featuring Grenada's Kéyòl speakers, please view the *Mwen Ka Alé* video at mariselagrenadelashley.com.

www.ingramcontent.com/pod-product-compliance
Lightning Source LLC
Chambersburg PA
CBHW052048070526
44584CB00017B/2110